# BUILT ON
# TRUST

## Gaining Competitive Advantage in Any Organization

ARKY CIANCUTTI, M.D., AND THOMAS L. STEDING, PH.D.

**CB**

CONTEMPORARY BOOKS

**Library of Congress Cataloging-in-Publication Data**

Ciancutti, Arthur R.
    Built on trust : gaining competitive advantage in any organization /
Arthur R. (Arky) Ciancutti, Thomas L. Steding.
      p.    cm.
    ISBN 0-8092-2446-1
    1. Organizational behavior.    2. Organizational effectiveness.    3. Trust.
I. Steding, Thomas L.    II. Title.
HD58.7.C53    2000
658.4—dc21                      00-24463

We would like to dedicate this book to Carole and
everyone at Learning Center who has supported us
through the years.

Interior design by Rattray Design

Published by Contemporary Books
A division of NTC/Contemporary Publishing Group, Inc.
4255 West Touhy Avenue, Lincolnwood (Chicago), Illinois 60712-1975 U.S.A.
Copyright © 2001 by Arthur R. Ciancutti and Thomas L. Steding
Printed in the United States of America
International Standard Book Number: 0-8092-2446-1
01  02  03  04  05  06  MV  17  16  15  14  13  12  11  10  9  8  7  6  5  4  3  2  1

# Contents

# Acknowledgments

ONE OF THE best experiences of writing a book on high-performance teams is working with creative people who have put so much of themselves into this project. We thank them not only for their direct contributions to the book, but also for being living examples of its principles.

John Anton, Marjan Bace, Laura Baker, Nancy Bargine, Joe Canale, Steve Charrier, Dave Ciancutti, Johnny Ciancutti, Natasha Ciancutti, Dan Clark, Joe Colosimo, Carol Costello, Stan Davis, Blake Emery, Phil Evans (in memoriam) and the distinguished members of The Rueful Order, Sally Ewald, Candice Fuhrman, Scott Harmon, Linda Hayes, Lesly Higgins, Sharon Hume, Greg Jones, Debbe Kennedy, Don LaBelle, Larry Lossing, Dean Ludwick, Dan Lucas, Dan Lynch, Sharon MacFarlane, Jeff McClelland, Marleen McDaniel, Phillip and Elke McDougal, Bob Miller, Lou Muggeo, Mike Nelson, Margie and Jim Nunan, Ellen Pack, Mark Pecoraro, Mary Ann Peters, Brad Post, Michael Rothschild, Amy Sayre, Doc Searls, Jonathon Seybold, Martha Sintz, Anna and Doug Steding, John Steinhart, Del Still, Dan Thomas, Joe Tussman, Dennis Ventry, Scott Waldie, Wendy Wallbridge.

# Trust: The Quantum Competitive Advantage

TRUST IS MORE than a highly esteemed human value. Along with technology and innovation, it is one of the most powerful forces driving business today.

We are a society in search of trust. The less we find it, the more precious it becomes. An organization in which people earn one another's trust, and that commands trust from the public, has a competitive advantage. It can draw the best people, inspire customer loyalty, reach out successfully to new markets, and provide more innovative products and services.

You can intentionally *create* trust in your organization. You can drive a culture of earned trust that includes everyone in the company and harvests opportunities to increase growth, productivity, profits, and job satisfaction with virtually no cost to you.

In this book, we will give you a model for creating that culture, and show you how to work with its two most powerful components—closure and commitment.

## What We Offer

*Built on Trust* is about creating trust deliberately and systematically, using a proven model based on our combined fifty years of experience. You don't have to let your organizational culture develop randomly.

When a culture develops randomly, trust is rarely present—and the vacuum often fills with fear, greed, hallway buzzing, "Them vs. Us," and other negative dynamics.

We will see how cultures of fear and mistrust evolve in what we call "random organizations," and we will present antidotes to these conditions. We will explore such trust-based principles as consistent closure of issues and conversations, genuine commitment, and communication that is respectful and tactful. We will take you step-by-step through developing and implementing a set of Trust Model guidelines that reflect your organization's commitment to such ideas as growth, profitability, integrity, commitment, closure, respect, and responsibility. We will show you how to shape these guidelines specifically for your company, and how to use the process of developing, implementing, and maintaining them to build trust among your team.

IBM was one of the first major corporations to learn the value of earned trust. Over the years of their market dominance, they inadvertently developed a culture that punished sound risk that failed. Their people became very careful—more careful than they were creative. A bureaucracy grew up, partly based on a sense of entitlement. Innovation and mutual trust suffered. By the late 1980s, some people were as concerned with looking good to top management as they were with market performance. The result was that IBM nearly failed in the market. When they examined their culture, they discovered how much damage risk aversion had caused. Beginning in 1991, IBM developed risk guidelines that enhanced trust, and executed one of the most dramatic turnarounds in business history.

In this book, you will learn how to use one of the most powerful forces on earth—the ability to trust and be trusted—to generate a dynamic team culture that makes your organization more innovative and self-starting, less fearful of sound risk, and more competitive than you may have thought possible. Authentic trust can transform the work experience along lines that people are just beginning to imagine—and give you a competitive advantage you couldn't get any other way.

*Built on Trust* is for existing teams facing new challenges, for new teams in the process of being formed, for mature teams going through reorganizations, for already successful teams striving to be even better, and also for teams that are immobilized and may require entirely new strategies in order to survive. If you want the greater productivity, higher performance, and synergy of people working together toward genuine common values that bring a quantum competitive advantage in business, then this book is for you.

## The New Competitive Edge

Free markets demand that we keep our competitive edge. But to the business manager scrambling to keep up, Adam Smith's "invisible hand" often feels more like a clenched fist jammed into the small of his or her back. One after another, management theories emerge and capture our attention, only to fade from sight within a matter of months or years. They all have value, but they vanish as soon as they become established practice. More to the point, everyone has access to them and so they provide no one with a true competitive edge.

We have been preoccupied for most of this century with the notion of organization-as-machine. This model deals only with what can be observed, measured, manipulated, structured, and modified. Early fascination with time studies[1]—organizations as clocks and people as cogs—gave way to business process re-engineering[2] and time-based competition,[3] all essentially mechanistic perspectives on how to win in the marketplace.

Even our language reflects the idea of organization-as-machine. We speak of systems, hierarchies, structures, processes, and cycles. We step on the gas, take off like a rocket, turn up the heat, restart the program, and hit the wall. We seem trapped in a mind-set of externals, pursuing the management program *du jour*, trying to squeeze a little more blood out of something that looks increasingly like a turnip.

Current business thinking looks for a competitive advantage in the domain of the human spirit. In this new territory, we encounter meaning, trust, inspiration, depth, transcendence, and connection—as well as their dark-side counterparts of doubt, fear, conflict, isolation, and just plain feeling stuck. The search for competitive advantage is shift-

---

1  Robert Kanigel, *The One Best Way: Frederick Winslow Taylor and the Enigma of Efficiency (Sloan Technology Series)* (New York: Viking Press, May 1997).

2  Augst-Wilhelm Scheer, *Business Process Engineering: Reference Models for Industrial Enterprises* (New York: Springer-Verlag, 1998).

3  Philip R. Thomas, *Getting Competitive: Middle Managers and the Cycle Time Ethic* (New York: McGraw-Hill, 1998).

ing from the exterior to the interior and departing radically from the metaphor of organization-as-machine. It is looking into the spacious realm of the collective team mind for a new kind of resource.

Some striking case studies are emerging in this new realm. From Vermont, Ben and Jerry explain the philosophy that helped them build a multimillion-dollar international business on ice cream: "A values-led company earns the kind of customer most corporations only dream of— because it appeals to its customers on the basis of more than a product. It offers them a new way to connect with kindred spirits, to express their most deeply held values when they spend their money . . . buying a product you believe in transcends the purchase."[4]

The Trust Model combines the practical needs of the organization with the individual needs of people working in teams. It works both with the visible external systems and with the invisible emotional dynamics that are always in play when people work together—and it focuses this powerful combination directly toward trust. This is what gives Trust Model organizations their quantum competitive advantage.

Barbara was a senior vice president of product development in a Trust Model company. One of their Trust Model guidelines was that she could speak up if she saw that her CEO was making a mistake, or about to make a mistake. The fact that she felt comfortable doing so, and even felt an obligation to do so, added her intelligence and abilities to his—and saved the company from making serious mistakes on several occasions. It was a perfect example of an external, visible system being enhanced by guidelines for invisible emotional support that helped Barbara, the CEO, and the company succeed.

## Social Capital

People have only recently begun to study the role of social capital in business. Social capital is the emotional or psychological equivalent of financial capital. It represents something you can give to people, whether they are staff or customers. Social capital can take the form of trust, acknowledgment, appreciation, or the knowledge that in supporting you, they are doing something that is consistent with their personal values.

---

4  Ben Cohen, Jerry Greenfield, and Meredith Maran, *Ben & Jerry's Double-Dip: How to Run a Values-Led Business and Make Money, Too* (Fireside, 1998).

Francis Fukuyama examined the differences in economic prosperity among different cultures and concluded, "A nation's well-being, as well as its ability to compete, is conditioned by a single, pervasive cultural characteristic: the level of trust inherent in the society." In our current global struggle for economic predominance, he believes that "social capital represented by trust will be as important as physical capital."[5]

Robert D. Putnam builds on the notion of social capital as "features of social organization, such as networks, norms, and trust that facilitate coordination and cooperation for mutual benefit."[6] He examines differences in economic well-being in different regions of Italy, and traces success to an abundance or lack of social capital.

The same principles apply in individual businesses, and that trust represents enormous social capital with customers. We know that the social capital of trust works *within* organizations to create connections and cohesion among team members, which leads to greater productivity.

## The Trust Advantages

In the course of this book, you will see not only *why* a trust-based organizational culture produces extraordinary results and *how* to create this kind of culture in your own organization, but also some of the specific business advantages of being an organization whose culture is based on trust. Some of these are described in the following paragraphs.

*Enduring Competitive Advantage.* An environment rich in trust creates an engine for innovation. There is no upper limit to the combined intelligence and creativity of the team. The promise of trust is then extended to the customer, which makes for an extraordinary level of loyalty.

*Self-Regulation.* People at all levels of the organization are inspired to identify and resolve open issues without unnecessary or intrusive supervision by leadership, and to relate with one another in the framework of the Trust Model guidelines. People become committed to developing habits of reliability, follow-through, and clear communication.

---

5 Francis Fukuyama, *Trust: The Social Virtues and the Creation of Prosperity* (Tampa, FL: Free Press, 1995).

6 Robert D. Putnam, "The Prosperous Community: Social Capital and Public Life," *The American Prospect* Issue 13 (1993).

*Efficiency.* The Trust Model eliminates energy lost to suspicion, unresolved issues, forgotten commitments, unclear agreements, missed deadlines, and the associated propensity toward blame, gossip, resentment, and frustration. All of this energy then becomes available for productive use. On the connected team, somebody always knows when a particular issue has not been resolved, so you do not have to wait for the customer or the marketplace to show you that you are off track.

*Inspired Performance.* The connected team discusses and processes ideas at every stage, so incremental "fixes" and improvements can be made as needed. Ideas pass through many hands and are improved at each turn, so these teams have an unusual ability to create superior products and services.

*Capacity.* Trust-based organizations have a knack for holding opposite conditions and points of view simultaneously, with grace and clarity. They may, for example, have tight, structured, disciplined development processes and yet still be able to react quickly to changing market needs or internal situations such as mergers. The connected team is a crucible that can stand the heat and contain its reactions until a new synthesis is reached.

*Meaning.* Making trust a central principle anchors the organization in a set of values that everyone agrees is attractive and meaningful. People become part of something bigger than themselves—and that results in attracting the best people and keeping them happy and creative.

A culture of trust makes any organization more effective, more productive, more competitive, and a better place to work.

# Part I

# THE VISION

# The Leadership Organization

THE COMPETITIVE ADVANTAGE that trust gives your organization is there for the taking, waiting to be harvested. It's not even low-hanging fruit. It's lying on the ground!

**Leadership organization** is a phrase used frequently in business literature, and some people speak of leadership organizations that are actually based on fear or dominance. It is possible to lead by fear, but it does not produce the same order of results that we have seen in our work. By leadership organization, we mean one in which leadership consciously and intentionally creates a culture of earned trust based on closure and commitment. When people feel free and safe to contribute, you create win-win situations across the entire organization.

## Trust Raises Performance

If you have the courage and imagination to make yours a leadership organization, you can increase profits, productivity, and the fulfillment people feel at work each day without investing a penny. You can dramatically enhance both individual and organizational productivity, and gain a competitive advantage that is both self-sustaining and self-renewing. That advantage is alive in every moment, active in the spirit of the people who are doing and managing the work.

For example, Stan was a design engineer who was developing a hot digital product. As he worked, he realized that a certain new feature might make the product much more attractive to customers—and even expand the market. This was his dilemma: Should he, or should he not, run his idea for the new feature by marketing?

If he trusted the marketing people to respond objectively and competently, and to respect his desire to contribute even if they didn't agree with his idea, then he would probably run it by them. If he didn't trust that they would respond in this way, he probably wouldn't. He'd just stick to his job description, with the result that the company might lose an opportunity—or he would go ahead and implement the feature on his own, without checking with anyone. The latter course of action might result in wasted time and effort if it didn't work for some reason, or if he were wrong about the marketing advantages.

In this case, an organizational culture that created trust among employees would allow Stan to perform more effectively, efficiently, and creatively. He could go to marketing, get the information he needed, and either proceed with the product or not—without either taking unsound risks or stifling his creativity.

## A Culture of Trust

The tool we offer for creating this culture of trust is the Trust Model. The Trust Model is an ongoing process of examining the specific areas in your organization that must be addressed in order to build a culture of trust—these might include growth, profitability, closure, commitment, communication, speedy resolution, respect, and responsibility—and, within that process, creating and continuously updating your own customized set of Trust Model guidelines. These guidelines give people a framework for interacting with one another and with your stakeholders in ways that foster and reward trust, and that bring you the benefits of being a leadership organization.

This book takes you step-by-step through the Trust Model process. You will learn exactly how to develop your own Trust Model guidelines, and how to bring them to the organization for everyone's input and buy-in. You will see that being an organization in which people trust one another, and one that is trusted by its customers and stakeholders, gives you a competitive edge that can't be duplicated or equaled. This competitive advantage is reflected in earnings, markets, innovation, efficiency, customer satisfaction, morale, reputation, and the ability to draw the best people in your field.

Two essential elements in any Trust Model are closure and commitment. Closure simply means that each time people come together to get something done, everybody knows who is going to do what next, and by when. Commitment means that when people say they will do something, they aren't saying "I think I will do it," "I hope I will do it," or "I'll try to do it." They are making an unconditional promise for action—not necessarily an unconditional guarantee of the outcome, but a pure intention to keep their word.

When companies do not intentionally create a clearly defined organizational culture, they become what we call **random organizations**. In random organizations that do not consciously drive a culture of trust, fear moves in to fill the void. "Them vs. Us" quickly becomes the primary way that people interact with one another. People's first concern is defending their territory. They start working against one another instead of with one another. They are driven by fear, rather than by a vision for themselves as individuals and for the organization, resulting in obvious costs in wasted time, energy, productivity, effectiveness, and morale.

Leadership organizations can sidestep this dynamic. Trust Model guidelines based on authentic commitments and consistent closure move your organization in the direction of trust. "Them vs. Us" becomes the exception, rather than the rule, and everyone's energy can be used in more positive ways.

The clarity and focus that come from consistent closure and genuine commitment are the very foundation of a trust-based organization. When people know who is going to do what, by when, and that people mean what they say, then they can trust one another. There may be slippage from time to time, but even handling the slippage is part of your Trust Model process.

To see exactly how the Trust Model gives you this competitive advantage, we will first look at how teams really work, and at why some are more successful than others. We will explore how "Them vs. Us" and other negative, fear-based dynamics emerge, grow, and spread when an organizational culture is allowed to develop randomly. We'll see what it costs you, and what you can do about it. We will show how closure and commitment counteract these negative dynamics and provide the foundation for productive, vision-based teams. We will give you simple, powerful principles for creating an organizational culture based on closure and commitment, and five steps to getting buy-in for your Trust Model guidelines at all levels of the organization.

Finally, we will see not only that you *can* drive a culture of earned trust, but that you *must* do so in order to compete.

It all starts with teams, with people coming together to get something done.

*coming together to make a positive impact*

## What Really Happens on Teams?

The minute you interact with another person, you are part of a team— whether the interaction involves a casual hallway encounter or a huge merger, whether the person is a custodian or the CEO, whether the interaction is through electronic media or face-to-face, whether you are dealing with one person or with thousands. As soon as you make contact, you're on a team.

Not only that, but every interaction has an outcome—and that outcome matters. Every outcome has an emotional impact. We feel more or less productive, more or less happy and satisfied, as a result of every interaction we have with others. The emotional impact may be large or small, but each time we interact with someone at work, the outcome will be more successful or less successful, depending on two things:

1. **Did the interaction come to closure?** That is, does everybody know exactly who is going to do what next, and by when? John finds out on Monday morning that he will be managing an emergency project for one of his advertising agency's clients, a clothing manufacturer now under fire for overseas labor practices. They want a countercampaign "yesterday." John meets with the client, the art director, the copywriters, and the president of his agency to determine the nature of the ads, where and when they will be placed, and timelines for the writers and artists. Everybody leaves knowing that they will have to work hard to meet the deadlines, but absolutely clear about who is going to do what, and by when, to produce the desired result. They may feel under the gun, but they don't feel confused. They won't spend any energy wondering which direction to take, or worrying about who is handling the other parts of the project.

Compare this result with an alternative. John meets with the client, the president, the art director, and the writers. They machinate about the unfairness of the attack and what should be done to counteract it. Many possibilities are suggested, but they don't come to many conclusions. Finally, after three hours, the client and president seem to bless a general direction, but the meeting adjourns without clear decisions, task assignments, and due dates. Everybody leaves feeling incomplete, and likely to spend a lot of time and energy wondering and worrying about what will happen.

John may come up with a more specific plan by himself, but he doesn't know if the president and client will approve. He either has to go off on his own and hope for the best, or reopen the conversation with them later and hope they will agree with whatever he suggests. And until one of those things happens, the art director and writers are left hanging—knowing that everything is due "yesterday," but unable to start working.

This latter scenario leads to frustration, resentment, withdrawal, and lack of productivity. The first scenario, in which closure was reached, leads to certainty, productivity, and a synergistic result.

2. **Did that closure result in some degree of success for everybody involved?** The first person you want to succeed is your client or customer, but it's important that everybody involved feel some level of success. The art director and writers may not like their deadlines, but they will feel successful when they meet them. John may not like working on emergency projects, but he does get to wear a white hat and be a hero. The agency president will look great when they get the campaign up and running, and the client will have a great countercampaign.

Closure helps create successful team interactions. This is important not just because successful team interactions produce good results, but because they create a positive emotional atmosphere. Teams are essentially emotional environments. We all have feelings about the outcomes of our interactions, and we make decisions about our future behavior based on those feelings. People's instincts, gut reactions, emotions, and intuitions are at the very core of team dynamics. They are at least as important to a team's productivity as the structures of the organization or meetings, although these structures can be a help or hindrance.

A culture of trust focuses all these emotional interactions and relationships in productive ways. When people feel supported and valued, they can give their all and make the contribution they want to make.

Let's look more closely at what we mean by "organizational culture."

## Your Organizational Culture

Culture is what is considered "cool" in any given environment. When smoking cigarettes was cool, a lot of people smoked. Now, at least in California, smoking is not cool. People are rarely allowed to smoke in offices, homes, restaurants, and even bars because it is considered offensive and dangerous to the people around them. They have to go outside if they want to smoke, regardless of the weather or the neighborhood.

But for decades, this was not the case. In the 1940s and 1950s, smoking was cool. If you didn't smoke, you weren't cool. You wouldn't have adventures or romance, wouldn't be an independent, sophisticated, powerful person. People have suspected since the 1930s that smoking is one of the most dangerous things you can do with your health, and the information that nicotine was an addictive poison was made public in 1953. Still, smoking didn't start to decrease until the mid-1980s, when it stopped being cool. For decades, people actually died in order to be cool.

Organizational culture is what's cool in the organization. We've seen in many hot new start-up companies, for instance, that the cool thing is to say "Yes" right away, no matter what is asked of you. It's not cool to say "No," or even to negotiate a better solution, regardless of how impossible or ill-conceived the request is. People don't dare stop to consider whether or not the request is actionable; they just say "Yes" with no idea of how they're going to get it done. In this kind of atmosphere, relationships quickly become strained and unproductive—with the inevitable costs in profit, time, esteem, energy, and satisfaction.

When the organizational culture moves toward trust through closure and genuine commitment, everybody wins. People know how to create certainty for themselves and those around them. They know what is happening, and they have the tools to maintain and expand that certainty. They make sure that responsibilities for each part of the job are clearly assigned, that they and others mean what they say, and that slippage is handled in a clear and respectful way. Everybody begins to see firsthand the answer to the question: Which is the strongest motivator—fear or trust?

## Fear or Trust: Which Is More Powerful?

Many corporations have used fear to keep employees "in line" and "on their toes." They have overtly or covertly encouraged people to compete with one another so that they "stay sharp" and keep in "hunting trim." But more often than not, they find that this philosophy reaches a point of diminishing returns very quickly.

Jim was president of a subsidiary of an eastern high-tech organization. He had a strong personality, and a very strong ego. He ran his ship without help, using liberal doses of fear and intimidation. Senior personnel at the parent company called him "Old John Wayne," but never to his face. People who reported directly to him resented him, and people at the parent company were intimidated by him, but his style was overlooked because he produced great results. His habitual response to inquiries was, "Everything's fine. If you don't like the profits, sell us!"

Gradually, the abyss between the subsidiary and the parent company widened. Jim's staff stopped questioning him, and was afraid to report information that was "bad news." This meant they couldn't deal with changing market conditions, or with the warning signs that were beginning to surround the business's highly volatile financial transactions. The result was a mixture of financial disasters and ugly behaviors.

Many of the people around Jim had been waiting and hoping for his downfall. When his soft underbelly was finally exposed during these difficult times, they seized the opportunity to "get him," and he was eventually fired. It took four years of diligent effort to overcome the residual attitudes created by his reign of terror and turn the company around so that it succeeded.

We have seen over and over again that trust releases productive energy within an organization in ways that are not possible in fear-driven organizations. Trust is a far stronger, and more reliable, motivator than fear. To keep our competitive edge, we need to innovate. To be innovative, we need to work in an environment in which we trust and are trusted.

In the presence of trust, people can tap into the power of true teamwork. On teams bound together by an overarching set of trust principles, the lines of communication are consistently open. Contributions are given and received readily, and there is an assurance that at least most of the members are "for" one another. Earned trust, rather than fear, is the binding agent for this kind of team. We call it the connected team.

## The Connected Team

The connected team combines not only the intellectual assets of individual participants, but also their instincts, hunches, dreams, aspirations, creative imaginings, gut reactions, musings, and moods. In a safe environment of trust and respect, people are free to bring these gifts to the table. When everybody feels free to contribute *all* their resources, they create a larger network of intelligence. Everyone's contributions are gathered up, unified, and synergized toward a common goal.

This is exactly what happened at one high-tech Silicon Valley company. Secrecy from competitors had become so important that a culture of secrecy had grown up *within* the organization. The secrecy gave rise to severe "Them vs. Us" dynamics throughout the company—but especially in research and development. R&D's performance plummeted, crippled by rampant "Them vs. Us" dynamics both within their own group and with other departments. At this very point, the market demanded that R&D become the lead group in the company. Just when their ability to perform was at its lowest, they needed to be at their peak!

Suddenly, management's fear of losing market share became greater than its fear of losing secrets. The CEO called a meeting with R&D and asked for help in finding a solution to the secrecy and "Them vs. Us" squabbles. His courage and honesty had an electric effect. Everyone saw immediately how the "Them vs. Us" dynamic had developed, and how disastrous the effect had been.

Management worked with R&D to devise ways for R&D to optimize their creativity and still preserve secrets. Within weeks, they found specific, effective ways to share ideas. The plan included ways to work new employees, who were seen as the greatest security threats, into the system without real risk. The two connected teams—management and R&D—worked together, bringing all their resources to bear on the solution. A higher order of creativity helped them keep their place in the market, and also made the company a much better place to work.

Connected teams enjoy another advantage as well. They experience an exponential boost whenever new members are added. When new people come into an environment where fear is dominant and connections among team members are weak, the team intelligence increases only by what that one person brings to the table. Add another member, and you get only his or her individual potential added to the team. But when trust is pervasive, as it is on connected teams, then communication is full and open. Emotional reinforcement is generous, and people are committed to resolving issues quickly. When you add new team members or reorganize teams under these circumstances, the group intelligence grows exponentially. People interact in ways that create an upward spiral of creativity. Ideas are exchanged quickly and easily, and improved continuously. The whole becomes greater than the sum of its parts.

The connected team represents team life in its highest, most creative, and most efficient state. Connected teams created within the Trust Model are not just another management fad providing a new form of competitive advantage; they are part of a process that can *keep* creating new forms of competitive advantage forever. The Trust Model becomes the *generator* of technique, not the technique itself. It integrates the raw intelligence and creativity of individual team members into a new synthesis that operates on a much higher plane.

## Why Trust Works

The principle behind the leadership organization, with its connected teams, is that people have a natural inclination to give. In fact, we have found in our combined fifty years of working with people that everyone has a passionate desire to contribute. We have a hunger to be part of something bigger than ourselves, especially when that something bigger reflects and amplifies our inherent values. This desire is a primary emotional need at work, and it must be satisfied if we are to be productive and happy in our jobs.

Opposing the urge to contribute and participate is fear—fear of rejection, failure, loss, retribution, or embarrassment. Sometimes we hang in the balance, afraid to go this way or that. It's as if we're standing at the end of a diving board, not wanting to jump and not wanting to climb back down.

People's passion to contribute may not be obvious when you first walk into an organization, especially if a random culture has grown up that does not ask or even allow them to bring their best to work. But scratch the surface and you will find that people want to be productive. They want to help and serve. They want to know that the world is a better place because of what they did each day. We have found that, when we get down to the truth, motivation is almost never the problem.

The problem arises when people think that their opportunity to contribute has been thwarted. The thing they want most is no longer available to them, or so they think, and so they withdraw, become defensive, gossip, cause trouble, or start just going through the motions at work. We worked with one small company that had recently been acquired by a giant. The people there felt thwarted when they were no longer allowed to make the good decisions that had produced their success in the first place. Mary, the vice president for research and development, stopped bringing her best ideas to her boss after she felt a couple of them were ignored. The rest of her team followed suit, and that set the standard until they were able to reverse this dynamic.

Suppose you have a great idea for a product and want to take it to the board, but you are afraid some board members might object to it. You go back and forth, deliberating about when, where, or if you should bring it up. Eventually, you take the idea to the board. They don't seem very interested, or even very conscious. They interrupt your presentation, and you can tell by their questions that they're not really listening. It's not even that they disagree with you; they just don't seem to be engaged. How would you react? Or suppose you present your idea to the board, and they are completely opposed to it. People ridicule you, and all your worst nightmares about rejection and failure seem to be coming true. How would you react then? Or suppose they love the idea! You are now the organization's new genius, the rising star who can do no wrong.

Your responses to these different scenarios may range from frustration to elation, but your reaction will always be *emotional*—and it will be based on how well your desire to contribute, and the risk you took to make that contribution, were received. Our passion to contribute is always balanced against our instinct to protect ourselves—and there is an important emotional consequence, positive or negative, each time we take the risk to contribute and be productive.

This passion can be our greatest asset, or our greatest vulnerability. It is our greatest asset when it impels us forward to use all our talents to help and serve. It is our greatest liability when we are thwarted and feel the pain of failure or rejection. True leadership knows how to make our passion to contribute an asset most of the time.

## Feeding the Passion to Contribute

In a leadership organization that drives a culture based on closure and commitment, people are rarely thwarted in their desire to contribute. Their proposals may not always be accepted, but they are treated with respect. People are valued for their ideas and their willingness to take the risk, whether or not those ideas are actually implemented. Their passion to contribute is recognized, valued, and encouraged.

When we stand poised between our genuine desire to serve and be productive, and our fears about rejection or failure when we reach out to make that contribution, what tips the balance is *trust*. If we work in an environment of trust, and one in which leadership models trust, we feel reinforced, validated, and supported. We are more likely to plunge in and put more of ourselves into our work. We are far more likely to be creative and generous with our talents. An organizational culture of trust makes us *want* to support and contribute to the company.

In a random organization, on the other hand, the ability to contribute is hit-or-miss. Sometimes people can contribute and feel great. Other times, they wish they'd never opened their mouths. Nobody really knows how it will turn out, because nobody is in charge of setting an emotional direction for the organization. There is no one to tip the balance in favor of contribution by consciously creating an environment of trust and respect.

Carmen was recently recruited from her position as senior vice president of sales for a cable TV station, where she was a seasoned and celebrated success, to a similar position in an emerging Internet company. Everyone assumed she knew exactly how to build a sales force in this new medium, but she didn't. In fact, everyone in Internet sales was a pioneer. No one really knew how to sell ad space on the Internet. This was Carmen's dilemma: Should she admit she didn't know what to do and ask for brainstorming help from her fellow executives, or should she continue to bluff and tough it out?

Which do you imagine would be more productive for the company? The rational answer is obvious, but the emotional environment could make it difficult for her to execute. If she could ask for help without fear of people judging or denigrating her, Carmen would have considerably more resources available to her. She could access the combined experience and intelligence of the connected team, use them to network into other sources of information, and certainly do a better job of building and directing her sales force.

A trust-based culture protects people's ability to contribute and gives them an environment in which they can bring their best to work without undue fear of consequences. These are essential emotional elements in any productive work environment.

## Creating Trust Quickly

One reason the Trust Model produces extraordinary results is that it is designed to meet trust on its own terms, and to work with the very nature of trust.

Trust is a dual concept. It has both a feeling or *emotional* component, what *Webster's* calls "assured anticipation; confident hope," and an *intellectual* component. This intellectual component is based on a track record of performance that confirms trust, or "assured reliance on another's integrity, veracity, justice," etc. The *active* result of trust is confidence—in the honesty and reliability of the company's leadership. The *passive* result is the absence of worry or suspicion.

Trust, then, is confidence and the absence of suspicion, confirmed by the track record and our ability to self-correct. The Trust Model not only covers all these bases—emotional and intellectual, active and passive—but it also works quickly, which is essential for success in the marketplace.

We know that it can take up to two years to establish trust between individuals. This is why we reserve our greatest trust for our most established relationships—our family, our long-term friends, and our social circles. But in business, we are in a hurry. Time is of the essence. Two years includes eight financial quarters, more than enough time to perish in the current economic climate. We need something faster and more efficient.

The premise behind the Trust Model is that *people are willing to trust more quickly when principles that promote trust have been explicitly and universally adopted by the team*. And they are willing to continue that trust for as long as people's behavior, particularly the behavior of key leaders, is consistent with those principles. Provisional trust, confirmed by experience, then deepens into institutional trust.

So rather than waiting two years to establish trust among the team, the Trust Model lets you establish a substantial level of trust in only a few weeks, the time it takes to develop your particular adaptation of the Trust Model and a short period in which people watch others (especially the leaders) demonstrate their adherence to it.

## It's "Bigger than Any of Us"

For the Trust Model to work this quickly and effectively, it has to be "bigger than any of us." No one in the organization can be above it, even and especially the leadership. People know the Trust Model is working when trust is more important than any personality, no matter how charismatic, in the organizational culture.

We build into the Trust Model evaluations that are frequent and include *everybody*. These evaluations are objective, explicit, open, and not easily evaded. In fact, evasion *defines* noncompliance, especially when it is attempted by leadership. Since there is no hiding, the team quickly understands exactly how committed the organization is, or is not, to trust as a central principle. The Trust Model even provides a screening process for selecting new team members, since it clearly defines how the organization will conduct its business.

One CEO of a recently successful Trust Model start-up, for instance, always spent about an hour with prospective employees just talking about trust principles—closure, commitment, communication, speedy resolution, respect, and responsibility. People were always surprised when he spent so much time talking about these principles, rather than about specific job responsibilities, but the result was that he hired people who were committed to trust concepts and who were on the same page with one another and with the company. People who worked at the company enjoyed an extraordinary level of unity, because they all thought the same way about trust. They became a community that is still a close personal network, even though many of them have gone on to different companies.

## Harvesting the Diversity of Teams

Leadership organizations also use their culture of trust to make diversity a source of higher intelligence, rather than a source of conflict.

In today's business world, teams are likely to be quite diverse. People on any given team may be at different levels of the organization or responsible for different functions. They may even be in different geographic locations. They almost certainly have different incentives, priorities, agendas, and points of view.

Even people who understand the advantages of diversity can succumb to fear and allow these differences to degenerate into "Them vs. Us" dynamics. Is the answer to make teams more homogeneous, to put together people with more similarities than differences in order to avoid conflict? Absolutely not. The answer is to *use* the tension, conflict, and diversity to create a higher order of intelligence on teams.

In an atmosphere of trust and support, different points of view can be expressed openly and safely. People feel free to speak their minds and contribute their unique wisdom without fear of recrimination or ridicule. This gives the team access to more information and more energy. Leadership organizations harvest the exponential intelligence that diversity affords them, and use it to create their competitive advantage.

## The Ultimate Advantage

The skills involved in creating a leadership organization are *learned*. With the principles in this book and a little practice, you can lead your team toward a culture of trust—whether your team is the entire organization or a few coworkers.

Leadership is more an emotional challenge than an intellectual one. Most of us already know what needs to happen next in our organizations strategically and logistically, or we can figure it out pretty easily. The real task of leadership is to provide an emotional environment in which people feel valued, satisfied, and certain as they contribute their talents and abilities. That leads to higher productivity, greater personal happiness, and an intelligence that increases with the diversity of the team.

As a leader, you actually have two challenges. The first is to model trust, closure, and commitment yourself, so that people have confidence in you as a human being as well as a business leader. The second challenge is to earn buy-in from your entire organization for your Trust Model guidelines. Part IV of this book takes you step-by-step through the five phases of earning that buy-in.

If you don't take the challenge to become a leadership organization, you will be a random organization. We estimate that 90 percent of all companies are random organizations. They are almost always fear-based, reactive, obstacle-oriented, and dominated by "Them vs. Us," with all its negative financial, personal, and productivity consequences. In random organizations, closure is also random. Sometimes it happens, but usually it doesn't. There is no particular value placed on it, and people are given neither the understanding of its importance nor the skills to make it happen.

Leadership organizations, on the other hand, are proactive, vision-based, and service-oriented. Their leaders are people who forge new pathways, model the new behaviors of closure and commitment, and create environments that foster people's natural desire to contribute and excel. They also give people the skills, tools, and wherewithal to implement these principles. Leaders take risks, speak up, give their ideas, and encourage leadership in those who work for them. In leadership organizations, this type of leadership occurs at every level, from the CEO to the custodian, and includes all the stakeholders.

Being a leadership organization based on trust through closure and commitment gives you a competitive advantage that can't be matched or copied, and opens up new opportunities for intelligence, productivity, and profit. Your vehicle for becoming a leadership organization is the Trust Model, which we will discuss in the next chapter.

# Trust Model Principles

Trust-based leadership organizations have the power to support people in contributing their best, build vision-based teams, harvest the higher intelligence of diversity, and convert all this energy into innovation, development, productivity, growth, and profits.

You become a leadership organization by implementing and practicing Trust Model principles.

## Your Trust Model

The Trust Model looks different in every organization, because you and your team are always focused on your own needs and goals, but one universal result is a set of Trust Model guidelines that reflects your organization's vision and values. These guidelines make work richer and more productive because people have a clear and trust-based framework for interacting with one another and with stakeholders.

Most organizations' vision and values include growth and profitability. In this chapter, we will look more closely at some trust-based principles that you may also want to consider. These include closure, commitment, communication, speedy resolution, respect, and responsibility. You may have other principles you want to include as well. We focus on these because they relate specifically to trust, and because they may be new to some organizations:

1. *Closure.* Close all communications.

2. *Commitment.* Avoid false commitments.

3. *Communication.* Use direct and open communication.

4. *Speedy Resolution.* Clear up unresolved issues as soon as possible.

5. *Respect.* Use tact and respect in communications.

6. *Responsibility.* Own your own problems, but be willing to give and receive help.

We will also offer some corollary principles that you may find useful.

Your Trust Model guidelines are framed and modeled by leadership and then offered to the entire organization in a systematic way for everyone's input and buy-in. People at all levels of the organization participate in developing and shaping them. Building your guidelines requires everybody's involvement, contribution, and creativity—and the process of drafting your guidelines, communicating to the organization about them, earning acceptance for them, and maintaining and evaluating your Trust Model are all part of that trust building. (We will show you in Part IV exactly how to develop and implement your Trust Model.) The Trust Model is truly a process, not just a set of rules.

Following are a few of the principles you should consider in formulating your Trust Model guidelines.

## Area 1: Closure

Closure means coming to a specific agreement about what will be done, by whom, with a specific date for completion. You don't leave anything dangling. "I'll get you the report" isn't closure because there is no time given by which the report will arrive. "I'll do what I can" isn't closure because there is no specific agreement for what will be done. It's easy to see how lack of closure breeds uncertainty, hesitation, doubt, wasted time and energy, resentment, and lack of trust.

For example, let's say you are sitting in your office and Henry sticks his head in the door. Seizing the moment, you ask, "Henry, would you get me a ham sandwich?" Henry disappears without comment. You start wondering: Did Henry hear me? Is he going to get me the sandwich? When? Who will pay for it? Does he have the money? Or is he upset that I asked him in the first place? Does he remember that I got him a sandwich last week, or did he forget (which would be just like him)? Did Henry's mother teach him any manners? And what about the mustard!?

Lack of closure always leads to wondering, which takes time and energy away from other tasks. We sit and spin in place, going nowhere. Even if we try to shove the concern from our minds, it simply resurfaces later, perhaps in the middle of the night ("What *did* happen with that sandwich?").

When the situation involves the regional sales forecast instead of a ham sandwich, or a completion time for product development, or a response from our manager, the wondering quickly turns to worrying and the consequences are more dire. And the greater our passion for success, contribution, and satisfying the customer, the more consuming the worry.

Suppose you ask your manager for information you need to complete a project, and he gives you a "later" response such as: "I'll look into it," "I'll get back to you," or "I'll get it for you." You're left in limbo. Twenty-four hours go by. Is it too soon to call? You really need the information, but you don't want to bug him. Forty-eight hours go by. A week. Finally, you can't stand it anymore and you call him, only to discover that nothing has been done. Now what?

In a culture of closure, you can simply ask for a date by when he will get you the information. It's perfectly acceptable to meet his "later" response with, "Thanks, Jack, when can I expect to get the information?" If you still don't get an answer, a culture of closure actually asks that you persist, with tact and respect: "Can you tell me *when* you'll be able to tell me when?"

Then you can spend the time between now and that time doing other things—not wondering and worrying about whether or not you should call, whether or not anything is being done, or when it might get done if it hasn't been important enough to do up to now.

Wondering breeds suspicion, and suspicion is antithetical to trust. Therefore, *closure is critical to trust.*

The goal of a leadership organization is to have 100 percent closure on all communications, big and small. Imagine working on a large project with many small parts. Most people feel tension just reading those words. But now imagine that each task has a specific definition and a specific time by which someone has committed to completing it. Think of the freedom and energy you would feel, knowing that everyone has made a real promise to do his or her part. The team could then proceed with certainty toward the goal, and everyone could win. That is what happens when communications are closed.

When the marketing department of a graphic design firm asked product development for a completion date on a new, highly complex product, product development didn't duck. They responded with an overall target date, several intermediate "times when they could give times" depending on how the project was going, and what, if any, unanticipated twists and turns had to be considered. They also included a series of "choice points," or anticipated adjustment points when marketing, product development, and the customer could get together to make decisions about how, and how quickly, to proceed. This gave everyone the closure they needed to go forward, without saddling them with a rigid structure that could fall like a house of cards if one deadline was missed.

In a culture of closure, everyone involved in a communication is responsible for ensuring that it is closed. If you hear a commitment being made at a meeting without a date attached, for instance, you can step in and remind everyone to set the date. At first, before people start to experience the benefits of closure, you may get some defensive reactions from people who are uncomfortable with the new way of doing things. They might even say rather sarcastically, "Oh, you also want a *date*?"

Your answer is: "Yes."

Reaching closure is a fine art, which we will discuss in more detail in Part III.

## Area 2: Commitment

Commitment is an "intention of no conditions." This means that there are no hidden "ifs," "ands," or "buts." It doesn't mean that you absolutely guarantee the result that you promise, but it does mean that you enter into the commitment with every intention of fulfilling it. And if you discover that you can't keep the commitment for any reason, you speak up immediately.

When Roseanne developed the sales forecasts for the western region, she was committed to producing those numbers and expected to succeed. But by the middle of the third quarter, she realized that one of her assumptions had been inaccurate and that the actual sales figures wouldn't be as high as she had anticipated. She thought twice about speaking up because it had been dangerous to admit mistakes at the company where she had worked previously, but she also understood that to remain silent would undercut both the company's productivity and her own credibility. She'd had every expectation that her forecasts were accurate and that her commitment would be met, but when the situation changed, she knew she had to tell people. If she didn't, they wouldn't take her commitment seriously the next time. Taking a risk, she communicated her new doubts to the vice president of sales. They did some productive brainstorming and inventory adjustments that prevented unnecessary losses. Roseanne's position in the organization was actually enhanced because she spoke up.

## False Commitments

A false, halfhearted, or pretended commitment is saying "Yes" without the pure intention to produce the final outcome. When we go into an organization, one of the first questions we ask is, "How much of the time do you think people really mean what they say?" The answer is usually 20 to 60 percent.

False commitments can be made consciously or unconsciously, with or without malice. In most cases, nobody means to make false commitments; they are just one of our workplace habits. They are sometimes called "nodding commitments" or "hallway salutes."

"Sure, we'll finish that report by Friday. . . . It'll take a miracle, but we'll find a way. . . . Of course we'll meet the sales goal." In the mind of the person making the commitment and not following through, the false commitment may seem like no big deal. It was a lapse in memory, an excusable detour, an avoidance of the inconvenience of following through, or a change of heart—things everybody does, for heaven's sake! It's easy to justify not keeping the promise, but sometimes we forget about the consequences of the false commitment to others. The person to whom the false commitment was made, and who is still relying on it, is heading for a destination that will not be there when that person arrives. His or her reaction may range from irritation at the minor inconvenience of having to revisit the issue and establish a new commitment to there being absolute hell to pay.

The story about false commitments that immediately springs to mind is George Bush's famous "Read my lips" statement about not raising taxes. Fair or not, reasonable or not, justifiable or not, the drama that ensued when this false commitment was revealed may well have cost him reelection.

You may have experienced pretended or false commitments when people have said to you, "I'll get you the report," "I'll make it up to you later," "The check is in the mail," or "I'll get right back to you on that." If you didn't get the desired result, you were probably disappointed, angry, hurt, or simply less likely to trust that person the next time he or she promised something.

In an organization that winks at or even encourages pretended commitments, people stop believing what others tell them. They realize that what people say has nothing to do with what will actually happen. When they can't count on what others tell them, they try to stop caring. The trouble is, they can't stop caring. The passion to be productive and helpful still lives, even if it's below the surface. When we can't contribute, we hurt. We may disguise our hurt in ways that look cavalier, defensive, or even aggressive, but the pain of not contributing eats away at us and saps our energy.

We may even start making promises that we have no intention of keeping. We then start believing that we can't have integrity at work, because we have to say we'll do things we either can't do or aren't willing to do. We begin a cycle of not doing what we said we would do, then finding excuses.

For instance, an organizational culture in which it's not okay to say "No" always encourages false commitments. "Yeah, sure, I'll finish the artwork by Friday," people say, because it's what is expected of them. They know they can't possibly deliver what they've promised, but the culture dictates that they say "Yes" to whatever is asked. They don't feel good about themselves because they know they've just given a halfhearted or false commitment. They start to avoid the person to whom they made the promise and begin to gather evidence for why the inevitable slippage wasn't their fault. There must always be a "them" whose fault it was that the promise wasn't kept, so "Them vs. Us" is off and running.

"Of course we can have that ad campaign ready by May," Bill says, hoping that something—anything—will cause the deadline to be extended. He knows there is no way they can have the campaign ready, and moments after he makes the promise, he starts looking for reasons that he won't deliver the work on time. The trickle-down credibility problems begin to erode enthusiasm for the project throughout the department.

False commitments can take the form of simple nonclosure: "I'll get on it." A result has been promised, but the promise has no end point. When a date is attached ("next Tuesday," for example), we have closure. We can verify the promise's completion. By Tuesday, it will be done or it won't.

---

## FOLK THEOREM I.
*Every false commitment leads to unproductive
dramatization in the organization.*

---

False commitments bleed a team of energy in many ways. Each time a false commitment is made and the result is not produced, everybody has to expend extra energy. They first have to stop and figure out how to get the work done that was promised but not delivered. Then they have to fix the mess that they are probably in because the work didn't get done with the original commitment. They also have to deal with knowing there is someone in their midst who says one thing and does another.

The habit of making pretended commitments creates a downward spiral in organizations. People trust less, and fear more. False commitments may begin with the lead team, but they eventually work their way down through the organization to the customer. A customer who knows you make false commitments isn't likely to be a customer for long.

---

## FOLK THEOREM II.
*If you are learning about problems from your customers or
the marketplace, it is already too late.*

---

The worst-case scenario with false commitments is that they go undiscovered for a long period of time—say, until the first external measure of progress arrives. That could mean the first-quarter sales figures or the testing of the new software program. At this point, the false commitment is much more costly and time-consuming to correct. Not only have time and energy been lost, but it may be difficult to locate the original false commitment.

---

## FOLK THEOREM III.

*At least one person on the team always knows about a problem well in advance of it being revealed by an external measurement process or by customer complaints.*

---

We worked with a software company whose predicament illustrated Folk Theorems I through III. On August 19, this company shipped a "beta card" to a large networking company. The beta card was a very complicated product, and the customer had an internal delay of at least two months before they could start testing it. When they finally did the tests, the beta card crashed repeatedly. The customer was upset because the project was already behind schedule and threatened to cancel the order if the software company didn't make the beta card work within ten days.

The software company took them seriously and had engineers working around the clock to make the deadline—which they ultimately missed. But during the final press to finish, one of the engineers said, "They *should* be mad at us. That card was a piece of junk."

His comment revealed that as early as August, when the beta card was first shipped (and possibly long before that), somebody on the team already knew that it wasn't going to work, but hadn't told anybody. Somebody *always* knows about such a problem, and it's inevitable that, left alone, the problem will radiate out to the customer. At that point, it's often too late to fix the problem, and the result is lost energy, time, reputation, and business. If our software company had been aware that the card was "a piece of junk" back in August, they could have gotten to work fixing it during the two months that it was sitting over at the customer's office, not being tested. The result would have been a good product, less stress and overtime, and far less "Them vs. Us" among individuals and the two companies.

The software company learned from this experience and implemented several guidelines to help people avoid making false commitments. One of these was to relate this story to new hires and spend as long as it took to make sure everyone got the point.

---

## FOLK THEOREM IV.

*You can only honor commitments to customers to the extent that you honor commitments internally.*

---

False or pretended commitments are so common that we can sort them into categories. One category is "being late." Late to the meeting, late to the plane, late to work. Showing up late means that the person made a false commitment about starting on time. The drama, the wasted energy, the wondering, and the downward cycle begin immediately: "Where is Phil? Is this meeting on his calendar? Maybe we should check with his administrative assistant. He told me yesterday he'd be here. How are we going to restructure the agenda? Why is he always late? Doesn't he know that we're busy, too? Does someone have to be somewhere else after this meeting or can we extend it? *Does anybody give a damn around here!?*"

Another category of false commitments involves money. When we pay a lot of money for something but don't get the quality we expect in return, someone has reneged on their implied commitment. A small manufacturing business in Denver paid a huge commission to a well-known advertising firm to design a "deluxe" website. When the website failed to generate the "hits" that the manufacturing company expected, the ad agency responded by saying that their commitment was to beauty and design, and that they had delivered on those elements. The manufacturers didn't care about beauty and design; they were paying the ad agency to generate business!

Much of the frustration of everyday life can be traced to false ←— commitments. Bounced checks, late deliveries, shoddy work, unreturned phone calls, laundered shirts with missing buttons, poor work performance, broken partnerships, and so on—under close examination, all of these involve issues with commitments that were made but not kept.

An organizational culture in which people consider their commitments carefully, and in which they absolutely intend to do what they say they will do, generates trust. People can relax into their natural enthusiasm without fear that they'll be let down. That translates into greater commitment, greater creativity, greater satisfaction with work, and better performance.

## Area 3: Communication

When people communicate directly and openly with one another, the organization avoids or minimizes some of the most common communication problems: talking behind people's backs, withholding information, hallway buzzing, and avoiding certain subjects. It is also understood that people do not lie to one another, or even suggest that things are true when they are not.

Cal was the CEO of a large construction company that was enjoying a sudden burst of growth. In the flurry of new business, Cal developed the habit of making quick decisions with his CFO, Roland. He began excluding other lead-team members from critical parts of the decision-making process, and justified this exclusion "for public disclosure reasons." But the other executives at Cal's company began to feel like pawns. They had been cut out of the loop and began to think of themselves as victims, rather than as leaders.   Anoy ?

Some became subtly disengaged and started just going through the motions of their jobs. Others began putting more of their energy into resentment than they did into getting their jobs done. They developed an attitude of "They don't care about us, why should we care about them?" The organizational culture began to fragment. Time, energy, and opportunities were lost to worrying, complaining, and withdrawing. The company began to lose its dynamic quality, as well as the competence that had attracted new business in the first place.

The whole situation could have been mended, and the company reenergized, if Cal had called them all together, admitted what had happened as a result of his communicating exclusively with Roland, and promised to communicate directly and fully with them in the future. When Cal finally realized what it was costing him to withhold information, he became willing to change his behavior dramatically in order to get the company back on track. He began to model direct and open communication, and people were so appreciative that they made rapid adjustments in their attitudes and productivity.

Direct and open communication also means not talking behind people's backs. We sometimes hear that this isn't realistic, or that it's acceptable to talk behind someone's back as long as you have already said the same thing to the person's face. But even when you have already "said your piece" directly to the person you are now discussing with someone else, this activity wastes energy and can create ill will. The negativity spreads to the person with whom you are having the conversation, and from them to anyone with whom they may discuss the issue. It's much simpler just to adopt the policy of not talking negatively behind anyone's back.

Another objection people raise when they first hear about communicating directly and openly is that, in certain situations, it is not appropriate to divulge everything. These situations include trade secrets, strategies, pricing, and whether or not there will be a layoff. When we talk about this principle, we make a distinction between "telling all" and being truthful. Most people understand and respect the need for occasional and appropriate secrecy. This is different from withholding important information from another team member.

Another important aspect of direct communication is making sure that the "small voice" in the room is heard by everyone. David Whyte[1] describes the process of people finding their voice in social and workplace conversations, and notes that it can take time for some people to speak out with confidence. Often the best ideas come from the "small voice," the person who has trouble speaking out, and the leader must be persistent in order to make sure that this person is heard.

Most teams have far more wisdom available to them than they realize. When everyone is encouraged to speak, and openings are deliberately created for everyone in the dialogue, then *all* the ideas can be brought out.

Tom learned more about hearing the "small voice" when he participated in an organizational development exercise at the Sloan Pro-

---

1 David Whyte, *The Heart Aroused: Poetry and the Preservation of the Soul* (New York: Currency/Doubleday, 1996).

gram at Stanford Graduate School of Business. The class was broken into small groups and given a list of items. Each group was asked to identify which items from the list would be most important to have with you if your airplane crashed in the desert. The instructor said that certain people in the class might have an advantage in the exercise, notably a general from the Israeli Army, the chief anesthesiologist from the Stanford heart transplant team, a former Green Beret, and Tom, who had tank experience at the Desert Warfare Training Center in the Mojave Desert. These particular folks were organized into a separate group nicknamed the Afrika Korps so as not to bias the outcome. Tom's group knew that they were about to become an outlying statistic based on their superior knowledge.

As things turned out, they indeed became an outlying statistic. They came in dead last. Their group's discussion was more like a know-it-all contest than a discussion of the problem at hand. They were more invested in protecting their images as "experts" than they were in solving the problem. Any small voice that offered alternative suggestions, that wondered, that was open to alternatives, or that doubted didn't have a chance.

Exactly the same dynamic occurred when Terry, a lathe operator in a manufacturing company, suggested to the engineer that they needed to start using a new laser technology. His recommendation was met with a defensive silence. This nonresponse made Terry feel devalued, and he never again voiced ideas that might have saved the company money or allowed them to work more efficiently and deliver higher quality. Meanwhile, the company's direct competition did begin using the new technology and, as a result, pulled ahead of Terry's company.

By using direct and open communication, you not only eliminate serious and fundamental problems, you bring the team's full potential into play.

## Area 4: Speedy Resolution

A leadership organization addresses critical unresolved issues quickly and completely, so that people can gain closure and make commitments. Are we going to merge with the larger company? Will people be let go? Are we going public? What about the Christmas bonuses?

Unaddressed problems do not solve themselves. We all wish that time alone would resolve issues while we were off doing something else, but it doesn't. We need to become adept at identifying which issues have been left open, and at making sure they are closed.

When a midwestern utility company made some acquisitions, six senior human resources staff members were directed to move back to headquarters from their various geographic areas. This new arrangement meant that each of them had to make significant moves, uproot their families, and adjust their lifestyles. At least two of them had not bought into the new situation, but felt unsafe to say so because they believed the company operated strictly "from the top down." They thought they'd better shut up and toe the line, because they didn't get to vote, or even comment, on their situation.

In retrospect, when the company began implementing the Trust Model, a senior vice president noted that he had seen the warning signs. Well into the process, two of the HR managers had not secured housing in the headquarters area and were returning home every weekend. One of them "had to" stay in his original location to handle a number of "customer emergencies" and was "forced" to delay his transition. Two reported that while they themselves had bought into the new arrangement, their customers had not. The vice president said that morale in their divisions had plummeted, customer complaints had increased, and that there had been a great deal of unplanned turnover at senior levels. New and unexplained "Them vs. Us" arguments broke out among the executives. Seemingly solid promises were made in meetings, but the ball often got dropped and nobody really knew who was responsible. Overall closure reached record lows.

The vice president said that while he and others had seen all these clues, they were reluctant to address the problem for fear of upsetting the HR managers further. They hoped things would work themselves out with time. They delayed, and paid the price. They lost three of their best people and spent a great deal of time, money, and energy cleaning up the mess.

# Area 5: Respect

This principle simply means that people treat one another as they would like to be treated themselves—with dignity and respect.

Don't confuse tact and respect with "being nice." This guideline points to a deep, underlying, immutable respect for our fellow humans. It does not address the *content* of what you say to others. It doesn't mean you can only say nice things, or that you have to be sugary sweet—just tactful and respectful. Especially when you say uncomfortable things to people, things they may not want to hear, they are more likely to listen if you deliver the communication with respect.

Jeff was in the habit of approaching people with the directive, "We need to talk." He was unaware that this simple, honest phrase actually invited fear rather than the openness that he was seeking. When he changed to, "Could we get a few moments together?" people sensed that he was *inviting* and *eliciting* their participation, rather than *demanding* their presence or *threatening* their jobs—and they were much more receptive, even when they knew the conversation might involve difficult issues or disagreements.

It is also useful to make a distinction between necessary pain and unnecessary pain. Knowing a certain communication may be painful but is necessary to reach a greater good strengthens our resolve to move forward. When someone must be dismissed for a flagrant violation of the rules, we may not want to have the conversation—but we know we must.

Mel was a project manager who repeatedly refused to be held accountable for promises he had made. In two instances, he punished people for complaining to his manager. He was warned, but Harry, the director of his department, was reluctant to terminate him. Finally, after another flagrant violation, Harry let Mel go. Since Mel's entire section knew about the situation and the reasons for his termination, their trust in the organization actually grew as a result of his being fired. They knew the company meant business about keeping promises and other Trust Model guidelines. They understood that they could rely on being treated in accordance with those principles and that the company could be trusted to do what it said it would do.

Remember, teams are emotional environments. When people are not treated with respect, they are less likely to be productive. When they know that they and their ideas are respected, even in the face of disagreements, they are more likely to take sound risks and contribute from a position of high self-esteem.

## Area 6: Responsibility

In leadership organizations, people give and receive help—but in the end, everyone must be responsible for his or her own problems.

Some of us have been taught to be lone rangers, trying to do everything on our own, without help or support. In today's business climate, that simply doesn't work. We need to learn how to ask for and receive help, as well as to give it. You can get help without dumping the problem on someone else, especially if you remember the old standbys "Please" and "Thank you." And asking for help is not a sign of weakness. If anything, it's a sign of strength and productivity.

Melody Beattie's *Codependent No More*[2] reminds us that some people get locked into dysfunctional relationships in which one person is always trying to bail the other out of his or her destructive habits. The Trust Model is, in a sense, the antidote to organizational codependency. It clearly defines the rules for responsible relationships.

Betty was community relations coordinator for a large Chicago hospital and always showed up twenty to thirty minutes late for meetings with the administrative team. The president, Chuck, simply ignored the situation. This caused dismay and resentment among the rest of the team. They started showing up late as well, and complained about the length and frequency of the meetings.

Chuck realized that something was amiss, and finally recognized the impact that Betty's tardiness was having on the entire team. He also saw that she was fully capable of being on time if she wanted to do so. He addressed the situation head-on, with Betty and the team. Not only did meetings become more productive, but people saw that these kinds of issues could be addressed and remedied. They saw that Chuck wanted people to be responsible.

## Other Important Principles

The following paragraphs describe some additional principles that you may want to incorporate into your Trust Model.

---

2 Melody Beattie, *Codependent No More: How to Stop Controlling Others and Start Caring for Yourself* (Minneapolis: Hazelden, 1996).

*Be Responsive (Twenty-Four-Hour Rule)*. Consider including a guideline that asks people to respond to telephone calls, E-mail, or other requests promptly, even within twenty-four hours.

If you can't give a complete response within twenty-four hours, you can at least contact the other person within twenty-four hours and let him or her know *when* you can give a complete response. The other person may not get everything he or she wanted, but you've at least responded with a new proposal for when you *can* respond fully, and closed the communication by setting a new date.

Peter was a busy CEO and world traveler who was not always available to stop what he was doing and respond to detailed requests. Because he recognized how important it was for people to know when he *would* respond, he changed his voice-mail message from "I'll get back to you as soon as possible" to "I'll respond within the next day. If I absolutely can't get back to you in that time, my administrative assistant will call you with a response or a time by which I can respond directly. Thanks."

If people start seeing you as unresponsive, you invite trouble. A leading software company had a streak of intractable unresponsiveness in its culture. Outside parties tried repeatedly to get through, but their calls went unanswered. This nonresponsiveness continued over an extended period and was interpreted by some as the company's arrogance about their market dominance.

One company found it nearly impossible to work on a strategic partnership with this software group because they couldn't get responses from legal counsel that they needed in order to finish the paperwork. An important deal took nearly a year to put together, when it should have taken only a few months. They never worked with the software group again. Eventually the software company lost substantial market share. Their unresponsiveness to communication from other organizations was reflected in their unresponsiveness to market conditions, and they paid dearly.

*Handle Issues at the Lowest Possible Level*. This principle places the solution to most problems in the hands of those closest to it.

Scott, in sales support, had a dilemma about whether or not to grant a special exception requested by a field representative. His first step was, of course, to think about it himself. He couldn't come to a conclusion, so he brainstormed with his peers. This also ended in uncertainty. Next, he consulted his immediate supervisor. Only when the two of them couldn't find an answer did he get his supervisor's permission to consult the supervisor's manager.

Usually, the solution comes sooner than this—but Scott knew that he had done everything he could to handle the situation at the lowest possible level and so he felt fully justified in talking to the supervisor's manager.

*Tell the Truth.* Making truth-telling an explicit principle can be helpful, especially in organizations dominated by a "spin control" mentality.

In considering how to handle any given situation, start with the premise, "Just tell the truth." This helps people avoid the natural tendency to embellish, package, hedge, or equivocate. Joe asked Wendy in human resources a complicated question about his 401K, and she was embarrassed that she didn't know the answer. She knew he expected her to know, but the simple truth was that she didn't. Wendy had a choice. She could either try to bluff her way through, or she could admit the truth and say, "You know, Joe, I should have the answer to that, but I don't. Let me check with my manager and get back to you within twenty-four hours."

Not telling the truth is one of the most destructive acts imaginable in a trust-based environment. It demonstrates that the agreements about trust are less important to people than their own self-interest.

*No Surprises.* This principle extends truth-telling to a proactive principle. When new information is learned, good teamwork requires that we disclose it immediately to people who might find it either necessary or useful. Withholding information is one of the surest ways to destroy trust.

If Roseanne, our sales forecaster in a previous example, had withheld the new market information that cast doubt over her first forecast, she could have severely damaged her credibility—to say nothing of the inventory and monetary consequences.

*Management as Role Model.* In a company where certain members of the management team were expected to have difficulty understanding the importance of being effective role models, the Trust Model guidelines were explicit in stating this as principle.

Humor can help deliver the message. A corridor sign read: "Stamp out hypocrisy. Members of the management team who show flagrant disregard for the above will be burned at the stake. Subsequent infractions will lead to more serious measures."

At another of our client companies, the CFO repeatedly made false commitments in violation of the company's Trust Model—and those to whom he made them began to complain. The executive team addressed the matter directly and respectfully. The result was a simple system that made compliance with and modeling of the Trust Model part of the performance and incentive packages of every manager in the organization.

## Contract or Covenant?

These, then, are some of the areas you must address in order to establish an effective Trust Model—and some other principles that will probably prove useful. We have *never* encountered teamwork problems that could not be solved by adherence to clear agreements in these areas.

You may see the Trust Model as a contract between the management and the employees. We prefer to think of it as a *covenant*. A contract implies a *quid pro quo* agreement: You do this, and I'll do that. If either party fails to follow through, the other modifies what he or she does and is off the hook.

A covenant, on the other hand, is a sustained and sustaining promise that cannot be broken. This promise constitutes an agreement between all the employees, including management, and the company. It is, again, "bigger than any of us." It is woven through the fabric of your company, imbedded in your corporate DNA. And it outlives any single participant, for better or for worse.

Let's look now at the consequences of *not* consciously creating an environment of trust in your organization.

# Part II

# The Problem: How Random, Fear-Based Organizational Cultures Evolve

# 3

# "Them vs. Us"

"THEM VS. Us" calls up images of bad guys and good guys, of black hats and white hats—but these conflicts aren't about good and evil. They are simply about all of us being human in the emotional environment of teams and reacting negatively when our passion to contribute feels thwarted. "Them vs. Us" is usually the first dynamic to surface when people don't gain closure, and it can trigger a chain reaction of negative dynamics that reverberate throughout the organization.

"Them vs. Us" happens on every team—at work, at home, in relationships, in government, and even between nations. It simply means that there are two or more adversarial or disconnected elements on the team. Most of us get involved in this dynamic at one time or another, but teams that become truly great have all learned to minimize, or even eliminate, this condition.

To short-circuit "Them vs. Us" and create an environment of trust in which everyone is happier and more productive, we need to understand how this dynamic comes into being, how it works, and how it looks in all its disguises.

## "Them vs. Us" Happens Because People Care

If you walk into an organization in the advanced stages of "Them vs. Us," you might think at first that people just don't care about their work or about the company. But if you investigate further, you will probably find that this team, like most teams, started off with good intentions all around.

If you asked them what happened, you'll probably find that no one really knows—but over time an antagonistic atmosphere began to develop. People started to oppose one another and became polarized. The company's momentum slowed, and people seemed to fade away, as if their hearts and minds were elsewhere. They no longer volunteered their best ideas or voiced honest differences of opinion. Meetings became tedious, boring, and vaguely stressful. Only a crisis seemed to energize the team, and then only temporarily. Territoriality and credit-hogging increased. Buzzing became commonplace. People felt stressed and burned out.

The story is familiar to anyone who consults regularly with organizations. This kind of descent is so automatic, so fateful, so commonplace that it's tempting to conclude that it is simply inevitable. The prevailing attitude is often: "That's just how it is. Teams succumb to entropy, wind down, and wear out. To fix it, you have to bring in new troops, fresh meat, the next victim." Organizations simply begin to assume that they have to create disposable teams.

Arky Ciancutti, coauthor of this book, often addresses special business school classes filled with young, fast-track individuals from organizations around the world. These intelligent, competent people have trouble even imagining what their organizations would be like without "Them vs. Us." After all, they ask, doesn't moving up the ladder mean choosing the "right side" early in one's career, and then winning the war?

We believe that "Them vs. Us" is neither inevitable nor necessary. Most teams are not even aware of an alternative, but there is one. It begins with an observation that may appear at first glance to be counterintuitive—"Them vs. Us" occurs when people care.

---

### FOLK THEOREM V.
*"Them vs. Us" dynamics occur only when people care about the outcome of their work.*

---

The emotions ignited in "Them vs. Us" conflicts have their roots in people's passion about their work and their emotional reactions to the outcomes of their interactions with others. If they didn't care about their work or their interactions, they wouldn't be upset when they didn't reach closure and couldn't do their jobs well. "Them vs. Us" dynamics are simply the easiest and most accessible outlet for their frustration when they don't feel they can contribute.

In seminars, Arky often asks participants, "How many of you have ever been involved in 'Them vs. Us?'" Most people raise their hands. Then he asks, "How many consider yourselves positively motivated, and involved with the people at work?" The same people raise their hands.

"Them vs. Us" is not limited to relationships between people. It can crop up between divisions or functions of a company, between branches at different geographic locations, between management and staff, between contingents loyal to two different founders or leaders, and even between the company and its customers.

How does it happen that good, competent, highly motivated people with a passion to contribute wind up enmeshed in "Them vs. Us" and actually participating in a downward spiral? A series of very simple steps gets us to those bad feelings, and the steps begin when closure doesn't happen.

## Lack of Closure

We have seen that "Them vs. Us" almost always emerges through lack of closure. When we can't find out who is going to do what, by when, then we can't be as clear or effective as we want to be in our jobs.

When we cannot get reliable information on what is going to happen, by when, on important issues like salaries, marketing direction, deadlines, and areas of responsibility—or even on such smaller issues as when the sales figures are coming out—we feel thwarted and frustrated. We don't know what's happening, and we don't even know whether or not it's okay to *ask* what's happening. We know we're wasting time and energy on wondering and worrying, and that makes us feel even worse. And all of it has to be somebody's fault. It must be the fault of the person who won't give us closure, or the boss, or the company leadership, or just simply "the system." We want to blame somebody, and that somebody becomes "Them."

When this lack of closure is chronic and pervasive in our organizations, then the wondering, worrying, and frustration become ongoing.

Energy is continuously wasted, results are not produced, and we don't experience happiness or satisfaction at work. We are operating in the dark, and so all our fears about rejection, failure, being blamed, and somehow "losing" naturally rise to the surface. We begin to pull back and protect ourselves. The energy that might have gone toward producing extraordinary results begins to spiral down into a black hole of nonclosure, and we feel powerless to make things work.

That's when "Them vs. Us" rears its head. When Ray in marketing can't find out from Chuck in production when the product will be ready, he feels frustrated. He goes down the hall and talks to his buddy Bob. Ray's complaints remind Bob of his own problems with Rachel, and Bob goes down to the cafeteria and talks to Shirley about Rachel. Very soon, cliques have emerged and lines have been drawn. Ray isn't talking to Chuck, marketing isn't talking to production, and all the ancillary cliques and subcliques are simply accepted as part of the culture.

We worked with a manufacturer of sports equipment where the comptroller, Dan, was in charge of collecting proposed budgets from the various divisions in order to work out an overall budget for the company. He had all the information he needed except the numbers from packaging, which was a week late in delivering their projections. He called Jane, who was head of the packaging division, and asked what the problem was.

"I can't get what *I* need from the paper and plastic companies," she fired back at him, "and our head designer has been out with the flu. I'll have to get back to you."

Dan wanted to do a good job. He was invested in his work, both because he cared about the company and because he wanted to leave the office each day knowing he had done his best. His interaction with Jane was frustrating, and he found himself making up reasons why Jane was acting the way she was: "Well, maybe she's just as frustrated with those jerks at the paper and plastic companies as I am with her. She can't help it if the designer has the flu. She's under a lot of pressure, and she's had to travel a lot lately, so she hasn't been in the office. And besides, she's just a more laid-back person than I am. Maybe I'm too demanding." But no matter how good or bad the reasons, Dan still felt frustrated. He still wasn't able to do a good job with something that was important to him.

Dan was caught in the classic nonclosure bind: When we don't reach closure, nobody can win. When we can't win, our desire to contribute is frustrated.

Dan didn't sleep very well that night. He brooded over whether, and when, to contact Jane again. Should he call her first thing in the morning, or would that just make her angry? If he waited, should it be for a few days or a week? He tried to figure out how he could twist the budget preparation job around and insert Jane's figures at the very last minute. Even if he could do that, a week would be too long to wait. Dan came to no conclusions and showed up at work the next morning tired, upset, frustrated, and confused.

What does Dan do with his frustration? In leadership organizations, people know what to do with frustration. But in a random organization, nobody really knows what to do. More often than not, they do what Dan did.

## The Emergence of "Them vs. Us"

The next morning as he was getting coffee in the executive lounge, Dan ran into his buddy George, the head of marketing. George was a good listener, and Dan poured out the story about Jane. He told himself that they were brainstorming, but mostly they were "brainstorming" about what a jerk Jane was. In a leadership organization, where closure is an essential part of the culture and people have the skills to make sure it happens, Dan might have begun his conversation with George by saying, "Look, I'm having a little trouble reaching closure with Jane. Maybe you could give me some advice. . . ." But this was not a leadership organization, and that is not how Dan began the conversation. As he told George about his frustration, there was a little complaint in his voice, a little whine, an unconscious desire to get George to agree with him about how tough his situation was.

When it was George's turn to respond, he didn't help matters. In a leadership organization, George might have known how to convert that conversation into a true brainstorming session, with the intention for Dan to reach closure with Jane. But in a random organization, as theirs was, people are more likely to be reminded of the areas in which they themselves can't get closure, and to go into collusion with the complainer. That moves everybody even further away from a solution.

George commiserated with Dan and told him a hair-raising story about how Allen in accounting had done much the same thing to him regarding a new hire's salary. They agreed that it was tough to deal with that kind of laxness and incompetence. After Dan left, George found himself repeating their whole conversation to Christie in product development, and she had her own stories to tell about late reports from people "beneath" her in the organization chart. A lot of whining and complaining went on in the lounge that morning in the name of "brainstorming." The buzz had begun.

Buzzing can be loud or soft, depending on how hot the issues are and how invested people are in the outcome. The people involved are not bad people. For the most part, they are good, highly motivated people who are simply frustrated by lack of closure. They are us.

---

### FOLK THEOREM VI.

*All communication in the business organization boils down either to closing or buzzing.*

---

## Buzzing as Bonding

Buzzing is a way of bonding with other people, and bonding is a primary human need. Since buzzing often becomes the glue that holds people together in organizations, it can even become addictive. It often becomes the means by which people develop and maintain their connections with one another. These connections are one reason that buzzing becomes habitual. When George sees Christie again in the lounge the next morning, he'll think of their last conversation and ask her how the problem is going.

Buzzing is always problem-oriented. People in the buzzing group require problems in order to stay connected with one another. They are problem-dependent in their relationships, and so the team's energy comes from its problems. If one person tries to break out of this dynamic and establish trust with someone outside the group, he or she probably feels some initial disloyalty.

It's easy to identify problem-oriented groups. When you offer a new idea to this type of group, the first thing you hear is why it won't work, how hard it will be, and what obstacles are impossible to overcome. It doesn't mean that the people involved are negative; it just means that they have slipped into a "Them vs. Us" dynamic and that they are operating with a different focus from goal-oriented or vision-oriented groups. The consequences are distraction, wasted time and energy, lack of focus, inefficiency, and loss of creativity and initiative.

What happens in a problem-oriented buzzing group when the problem goes away—or is transferred, or fired, or gets sold, or even shapes up? What happens to the buzzers? Either they have to find new ways to interact (very difficult in a random organization) or they have to acquire *another problem*. If they don't, they have nothing to talk about and nothing over which to bond. Not only that, the next problem has to be *at least* as big as the first one in order to sustain the energy of the bonding. If there is no bigger problem around, the group will have to inflate one.

And buzzing is contagious. It spreads like wildfire. Instead of a problem-oriented group, you quickly have a crisis-oriented organization—an organization in which people depend on problems or crises to keep them up and moving. Just as the group needs problems, the organization becomes addicted to crises. In fact, people feel at loose ends without a crisis. And again, each crisis has to be bigger than the last. People get so busy putting out these fires that they eventually burn out.

## Wildfire

Meanwhile, it is only a matter of time before the people who are being buzzed *about* find out that they are the subject of less than flattering, less than empowering conversations. Sooner or later, we always hear negative scuttlebutt about ourselves—and we usually hear about it in indirect, exaggerated ways.

So, of course, Jane heard that Dan was "trashing" her. She was hurt, angry, and had the same negative reaction that most of us would have: "He didn't give me enough notice. He has his own issues going on, and he's trying to blame them on me. He's screwed up plenty himself. He doesn't care about packaging anyway, it's all just bureaucracy."

Naturally, Jane was not moved to spend much time in the executive lounge with Dan and his "colluders." Instead, she started hanging out with the guys in production—especially Les, who also happened to be friends with Allen in accounting, who was late with his figures to George. They agreed that the folks up in the executive suite were idiots, didn't really know what was going on in the company, and were just trying to protect their territory—mostly at the expense of the people who really made the company succeed, people like themselves.

Presto! A clique had formed in opposition to the executive lounge clique, and "Them vs. Us" was present in a full and virulent form. Both groups sought out people who shared the same priorities, difficulties, functions, frustrations, and responsibilities that they did—and both came together to buzz and complain about the other group.

Jane's reaction was not unusual. Very few of us would go right to the executive lounge and handle this issue directly. Most of us would unconsciously start to spend time with people who had the same sorts of challenges and frustrations we did, and who were "misunderstood" in the same way that we were. It's the most natural thing in the world, under these circumstances, to form cliques. There's "Us," here. And there's "Them," there.

It can be the executive suite vs. the plant floor, sales vs. marketing, the home office vs. the branches, the parent company vs. the acquisition, labor vs. management, engineering vs. operations, development vs. testing, Building A vs. Building B—any combination of individuals, functions, locations, interests, divisions, or levels of the organization. Here is a partial list of groups that are likely to develop "Them vs. Us" dynamics:

- marketing and engineering
- business development and marketing
- business development and manufacturing
- engineering and manufacturing
- sales and marketing
- sales and sales support
- finance and sales
- management of information systems (MIS) and everybody
- quality and manufacturing
- quality and engineering

- manufacturing and distribution
- manufacturing and packaging
- distribution and packaging
- human resources (hiring and firing) and project management
- facilities and engineering
- management and nonmanagement
- senior management and middle management
- senior management and other senior management
- senior management and the board
- the board and some investors/stakeholders

## Diversity: The Challenge of "Them vs. Us"

In today's business environment, most of us work with people whose incentives, agendas, perspectives, and priorities differ from ours. They may be at different levels of the company, have different functions, and be in different locations. With mergers and acquisitions, we may even work in what used to be different companies. Yet we depend on these people in order to do our jobs well, so the opportunities for "Them vs. Us" are everywhere.

Again, when we can't reach closure, we may come up with all kinds of reasons: "He's just crabby. . . . Their division doesn't care anything about us. . . . He's on salary and I'm on commission. . . . We're in different time zones. . . . We're growing so fast that I can't expect him to do everything." But none of those reasons give us any relief from the frustration—or make it any less likely that we will buzz about our frustration with those around us. If the people to whom we are talking are not trained to lead us away from buzz and toward closure, then "Them vs. Us" cliques get a toehold from which to grow and deepen.

Every person involved in the situation at Dan and Jane's company was positively motivated, smart, and competent. The only problem was that they worked at a random organization in which closure, commitment, and direct communication were not part of a clearly defined and universally accepted culture. The result was that they were crisis-driven rather than vision-driven. Over time, they lost touch with their passion to contribute. They started just going through the motions. They protected themselves and stopped taking sound risks. They stopped bringing all of themselves to work.

Nobody does this on purpose. Most people don't even do it consciously. Most don't even see themselves doing it. But the company suffers, and everybody suffers both personally and professionally.

People don't want to buzz or to be involved in "Them vs. Us." They would much rather be productive, connected, and contributing. In an organization that values closure in every single interaction and gives people the skills to create closure, they can do just that.

## The Cost

Some of the consequences of "Them vs. Us" are obvious. Time is spent talking, worrying, wondering, and complaining—rather than doing. Quality is affected in many ways. When people become problem- or crisis-oriented, when their energy is channeled against others in the company, and when they are scanning for bad news rather than good news, the quality of their work usually declines. Productivity and efficiency plummet, people withhold their skills and ideas, and the team becomes reactive.

All these things affect the bottom line, but "Them vs. Us" has an even more insidious cost. People start believing the excuses they make up for themselves or others. When we first fail to reach closure, we try to give reasons for the breakdown: "We're just too far apart on the map to work well together. . . . The company's too big for anyone to care. . . . Why even bother to try?"

Even more treacherous are the reasons we make up, and then internalize, for not doing our best: "Why should I work hard when no one else does? . . . They don't care about me. Why should I care about them? . . . I've done all I'm going to do. If they don't appreciate it, too bad. . . . Even if I did a good job, nobody would notice. . . . How can we be expected to lead the company's technology when senior management isn't investing (or caring, or thinking, or communicating, or allocating, or hiring, or whatever)?"

Almost instantaneously, these excuses turn into "the truth." In our minds, they become something we can bank on and a premise from which we should operate, if we're smart. It happens so quickly and automatically that we sometimes don't even see ourselves doing it. The farther away people are from the top of the organization chart, the less control they feel they have and the more you see these excuses.

Another serious consequence to organizations that become crisis-driven through "Them vs. Us" dynamics is that people start looking for direction not from the organization's purpose or vision, but from its problems. Where is the next fire they have to put out? What is the next obstacle? It's how they bond, how they get their energy up, how they express themselves. It takes a crisis to get and keep everybody awake. The problem is, it doesn't take the organization anywhere.

As devastating as nonclosure and "Them vs. Us" are to the organization, the first casualty will be you. You will feel as if people are not telling you how they feel, and you will probably be right. Your stress level will build and your motivation will erode. You will have less fun, or no fun at all. And the more you care, the more you suffer from not being able to reach closure.

All of this lowers the bar on quality, and the bottom line suffers.

## Finding Out Too Late

Perhaps the most significant cost of "Them vs. Us" is that problems don't get discovered early enough that you can do something about them before they reach the customer. Remember Folk Theorem II: "If you are learning about problems from your customers or the marketplace, it is already too late." That's when your competitors are hearing about *their* problems, and so you've lost your advantage. Most companies become aware of problems only when sales drop off, people stop calling, or customers complain. A leadership organization hears about problems long before this point, and can do something about them.

When individuals, departments, divisions, functions, locations, or other parts of the organization are not supporting one another—and may even be at war—then it's only a matter of time before that dynamic works its way down to the product or service, and from there to the customer.

If product development and operations aren't on the same page, mistakes will be made in producing the widget. If marketing and sales aren't on the same page, the promotion won't come at the best time to support the most sales. If packaging and distribution aren't on the same page, the product won't be ready to put on the trucks. If people aren't being cooperative with one another, they won't be cooperative with customers. If they aren't getting closure with one another, they won't get closure with customers.

So "Them vs. Us" is not only internal—between sales and manufacturing, marketing and sales, the home office and satellite locations, various layers of management and nonmanagement, senior management and middle management, middle management and supervision, supervision and the workforce itself—but external. Eventually, "Them vs. Us" manifests between the organization itself and its customers. And that is a death knell.

This particular consequence of "Them vs. Us" is completely avoidable, because there is always *someone* in the organization who knows there's a problem. In a leadership organization that promotes closure, the closure is for that person to say something to someone who can do something about it.

You may remember the story from the previous chapter about the beta card that a software company made for a major networking company. Months before the card had been shipped to the customer, and about a year before the final breakdown and ultimatum occurred, one engineer had known that it was "a piece of junk." In a culture of closure, everyone who heard that remark would have asked him exactly what he meant. The problem would have been discovered and fixed before the beta card was shipped. Many months of work and worry, hundreds of thousands of dollars, and a good deal of pride would have been saved.

Another serious consequence of waiting to hear about problems from customers is that the real source of the problem is often lost. At best, it's difficult to track back to what caused the initial problem. A "Them vs. Us" conflict may take months or years to work its way down to the customer, and looking for what really went wrong so you can fix it is like trying to find a needle in a haystack.

When the "Them vs. Us" dynamic in Dan and Jane's company ultimately finds its way to the customer—and it will—they may have no idea where to start looking for the real problem. In a culture of closure, Dan would have handled the issue immediately and directly with Jane. He might have said, "Jane, I needed those figures last week. If you can't give me an exact date by which I'll have them, could you please give me a time by which you can tell me when you'll have them?" The problem would have been clearly defined between the two people involved, and they would have worked it out on the spot.

When sales figures go down or customer complaints go up, most companies adopt a shotgun approach to finding and fixing the problem: "It must be the way we're advertising. . . . No, it's the mission statement. . . . No, it's all the new hires. . . . No, it's quality control. . . . No, we need a new website."

The worst-case scenario here is that one of their "solutions" actually works! If they get their market back as a result of one of these proposals, they may think they've actually solved the problem. But the real cause is lack of closure resulting in "Them vs. Us" dynamics, and it will be back—sooner rather than later. They think they've addressed the problem, but they haven't. The lack of closure is still going on. Problems will reappear, possibly in different disguises. The organization will deal with these problems only when they are in the crisis stage. Meanwhile, the organization becomes more reactive, more obstacle-based, more fear-driven.

In most cases, quality diminishes due to *internal* dynamics. No matter how much money we spend to find the external or structural problems, it's all about human beings interacting with one another—and we don't solve the problem until we address that. In a leadership organization, problems are caught as soon as they appear and solved through internal collaboration, team wisdom, and communication.

## Circumstances That Invite "Them vs. Us"

"Them vs. Us" will grow up naturally in any random organization, because no one is driving the culture away from fear and toward trust. Still, there are certain circumstances within companies that invite or exacerbate this condition.

*The Hot Start-Up.* "Them vs. Us" dynamics are common in successful, fast-growing organizations. High activity and excitement often obscure the real priorities of communication and closure. "We don't have time," is the message, and busyness becomes the justification for dodging communication challenges.

*Built-In Differences in Priorities.* When a group's inherent priorities, goals, or incentives appear to be different from, or even in conflict with, another group's priorities, the ground is fertile for "Them vs. Us" dynamics. For instance, sales is compensated by percentages, and so they are intent on gaining the highest *volume* of business possible. They have a natural, but often silent, clash with engineering, which is struggling with development difficulties and intent on producing the highest *quality*. Both groups are motivated positively and both are passionate, but when they get involved in "Them vs. Us," both are participating in activity destructive to the company's overall purpose, success, and customer satisfaction.

*Unproductive Bureaucracy.* The sheer boredom of lots of activity and little closure can encourage "Them vs. Us."

*Distance and Time-Zone Differences.* These can mask or obscure the problem of nonclosure. People can say that the problem with closing is logistics and trying to operate across time zones. In fact, it's more often procrastination or wanting to avoid communications that they anticipate will be uncomfortable.

*An Intensely "Political" Atmosphere.* When people watch their back and plot for the future, "Them vs. Us" is almost inevitable. In academic environments, for instance, counting favors and the fear of becoming indebted to the "wrong" person or department can justify this dynamic.

*Recent Mergers and Acquisitions.* When these changes are not properly managed and people are not given enough information, they fill the void with fears about losing their job, their comfortable relationships, or their territory. The result can be paralysis at exactly the time when you most need everyone's participation and support. Even after time has passed and "parenthood" seems to have been established, people can harbor suspicion and worries if the two cultures have not been consciously integrated.

*Authority in General.* Perhaps the most common circumstance that invites *a priori* "Them vs. Us" conditions is authority. For many people, authority brings up unreasonable fear even before they encounter the actual person who has the authority.

Subordinate/supervisor relationships are particularly susceptible to this dynamic. Institutional authority, authority that is yours simply because of the position you hold, has extraordinary power. Too often, people use the power of their position to intimidate others. And conversely, employees often place leaders on "pedestals of legitimacy" even when the leaders try to avoid it. Then they feel intimidated and whisper when the leader is nearby. Conversations stop prematurely when they see someone from management coming down the hall.

To be effective in authority, leaders must have people's confidence but not appear to revel in the power of their position. When the personality of the leader overshadows the role that he or she must play, people often feel threatened or intimidated. They feel at risk, and trust is lost.

Certain personality styles—in either supervisors or subordinates—are likely to invite "Them vs. Us." Some of them are described in the following section.

## Styles That Invite "Them vs. Us"

We can actually invite people to stop short of closure with us by adopting, or continuing to use, styles and attitudes that make genuine connection and communication difficult. These styles can be found throughout an organization—sometimes from subordinate to supervisor, sometimes from supervisor to subordinate, sometimes among peers. They all have in common asking for a special dispensation from direct communication and closure.

Sometimes we're aware of using these styles, and sometimes we aren't. See if you recognize any of the following styles.

*The Always-Decisive Style.* People who adopt this style have often had early career training that promoted and valued decisiveness. They were trained to believe that effective leaders are never indecisive. Now, years later, they always seem absolutely sure of whatever they are doing and never show a crack in their armor. They cannot bear to appear uncertain in front of the people they supervise, or to look weak by asking for help.

But these people are human, so they are actually unsure of themselves just as often as we all are—and everybody knows it. Neither their subordinates nor their superiors respect these people for hiding their indecision, and so often they don't volunteer information that they know would help. They figure that if Always Decisive wants it, he or she can ask for it.

The always-decisive style prevents us from using the combined wisdom of the team. When decisions emerge too quickly, without the chance for everyone to participate, contribute, and buy in, the result is often less than it might be. Staying connected with people and honoring doubt is sometimes uncomfortable, but it brings together the team's energy and thoughts, and produces a superordinate outcome.

*The Too-Busy Style.* This style belongs to the ambitious and consequently busy, but also to those who simply want to *appear* busy. People who succumb to the too-busy style create a flurry of activity around them and try to make it appear that all this activity means that a great deal is being accomplished.

People tend to stay away from Too Busy. When they do come around, they often get brushed aside like gnats who might cause irritation if they were allowed to land. Too-busy types can look like soldiers dug in behind their desks, just waiting for someone to cross the demilitarized zone and interrupt them. They are only interested in an "open-door policy" to the extent that they can get an earlier beat on whoever dares enter the office and disrupt the flurry.

In fact, few people dare to bother too-busy types with their small, insignificant little problems. Instead, they let the problems grow until they are out of control, or at least beyond the capacity of Too Busy. In so doing, they place their projects in a reactive mode rather than in a proactive one. By buying into this style, they place Too Busy's agenda above that of the team, and everybody loses.

Over time, Too Busys often forget why they adopted this style in the first place, and just do it now by force of habit.

*The Too-Nice Style.* The too-nice style is often a flag waved in surrender: "You don't bite me, and I won't bite you." Or it may be a smiling keeper, standing before a caged beast that he or she feels is just waiting to pounce given the slightest provocation. We tend to buy into the too-nice style easily because Nice is, well, nice. But oily assurances and conflicting promises eventually catch up with Too Nice. People start to realize that no matter what they say or promise, and no matter how nice they seem to be, nothing really gets done.

*The Mood.* Some people are dominated by their moods, and the folks around them have to figure out whether or not it is safe to approach.

Freedom from mood swings is a sign of psychological maturity. When we are possessed by a mood, we are no longer our real selves. We place our inner condition above the productivity of the team. The chances of gaining closure with the Mood are minimal—hit-or-miss, at best.

A close relative to the Mood is the Optimist, who exudes energy and enthusiasm even when all is lost. The Optimist is invested in the notion that attitude influences outcome. To some extent, this is true. Sometimes, however, the less buoyant of us have trouble staring into that kind of bright light.

*The Grump.* The Grump has one virtue that makes him or her easier to deal with than the Mood: the Grump is absolutely predictable. You know that talking with this person isn't going to be fun, and you know all the back roads in your building that help you avoid the Grump's desk. In your early encounters with this person, you may have attempted cheerfulness out of a natural urge to compensate for the gloom you sensed around the Grump. It didn't work, though, and now you know better than to try it.

*The Talker.* You may prefer a fast-food mode of communication in which you get in line, place your request, get what you want, and move along. But the Talker thinks more in terms of English teatime. You may want to talk business, but what you get is a long dissertation on the past glories of the Talker's particular empire—and you would rather just skip the meeting than go through that again.

*The Know-It-All.* Armed to the teeth with data and conclusions, these people overwhelm their teammates. Around them, most people are reduced to silence. These people can only focus on their own opinions, ideas, questions, and concerns. They never let themselves appear weak by asking the team for help. The results are less collaboration, less creative intelligence, and more re-work.

*The Tower of Babel.* You begin a conversation with this person and suddenly feel as if you are being hosed down with a stream of alphabet soup. Acronyms, jargon, technical terminology, and strange and foreign incantations fill the air. It is the contemporary equivalent of speaking in tongues. You start to look for a translator, but give up because it just seems like too much effort.

*The Medusa.* You begin a conversation, but soon realize that the purpose of the silence on Medusa's part is not to provide space for listening. Rather, it is a meditation on your stupidity. Your thoughts jangle, words fail you, and suddenly you realize you are turning to stone. You cannot win here, and the only thing worse than the silence would be for Medusa to say what is really on his or her mind.

These styles, attitudes, and conditions don't *cause* people to communicate incompletely, but they do invite nonclosure. Even in the face of the most daunting styles, some people will communicate effectively and persist until issues are closed. But many others will unconsciously accept the invitation to silence, or to appeasement, which reinforces their own habits of nonclosure. When this happens, individual agendas become more important than the welfare of the organization.

Being able to diagnose and name these dynamics in their early stages diminishes their power.

## Harvesting the Value

We have seen that "Them vs. Us" can crop up between any function, level, location, or element in an organization—between any groups that have potentially conflicting agendas, incentives, and priorities. It's important to remember that these dynamics are *opportunities*.

---

### FOLK THEOREM VII.
*The greatest prospective opportunities for competitive advantage arise from the most virulent current instances of "Them vs. Us" in the organization.*

---

Rather than avoiding the muck created by "Them vs. Us," connected teams strive to go *into* it in order to find a cure. One example of this kind of harvesting is "concurrent engineering," in which engineering and manufacturing work together from the outset to develop a product that both meets its functional requirements and can actually be manufactured. Engineering and manufacturing traditionally work in sequence, with engineering creating the product and then tossing it over the wall to manufacturing to figure out how to build it. Of course, this means that engineering can create products willy-nilly, without worrying about how to build them. Manufacturing then grinds its teeth over the "stupidity" of the designs. The resulting "Them vs. Us" dynamic leads to sarcasm and animosity. When this conflict is mined for gold, companies come up with "concurrent engineering," which works to their advantage.

Other companies establish cross-functional teams in which representatives from marketing, sales, quality assurance (QA), support, manufacturing, and finance sit on the product development team throughout the process and management stays out of the way. With representation from all functions, "Them vs. Us" is more easily eliminated.

By identifying the phenomena underlying "Them vs. Us," we can discover and develop sources of competitive advantage. There are an infinite number of ways to gain competitive advantage by looking beneath the tension in "Them vs. Us." So rather than avoiding these conflicts, leadership organizations use them to create a higher intelligence that discovers unique solutions. We name the problem, objectify it, and solve it consciously with a higher-level resource.

You don't want everybody to have the same agenda in an organization; you want all those different points of view, all those different kinds of energy working synergistically. A leadership organization knows how to harvest the benefits of that diversity through closure, commitment, and communication. "Them vs. Us" tells you that people *care*. When that caring is allowed to grow in the supportive environment of trust, it becomes a powerful force.

## "Them vs. Us" in Action

To illustrate how the Trust Model principles work, throughout the rest of this book we will follow two companies as they move through lack of closure resulting in "Them vs. Us." We will see them experience the consequences of being random organizations, and finally watch them implement the Trust Model in order to gain a competitive advantage in their markets.

These are fictional, composite companies, based on our experience with organizations over the years. Startup, Inc., is a small software development company in California. Bigger, Inc., is a medium-to-large manufacturing company based in Pennsylvania.

## Bigger, Inc.

Pat was the chief financial officer at Bigger, Inc. She was in charge of forecasting revenues and expenses. To do that, she had to get timely reports from all the divisions. Her nemesis was sales, and requesting these forecasts always precipitated a battle. Sales didn't want to comply because they got paid for generating sales, not for making forecasts. Further, they got paid based on expectations. If they exceeded what was expected and forecast, they got bonuses—so even when they did get their forecasts to Pat, their predictions were almost always minimized and deflated. The result was that she usually got inaccurate reports, and she got them late.

Pat had been with the company for twenty-eight years. She was close to retirement, so she wasn't exactly a firebrand, but she was heavily invested in having her division run efficiently—even perfectly. She toed the line and wished others would do the same. People who threw monkey wrenches into her system made her nuts, and she spent the whole weekend thinking about how Alex, the motormouth vice president of sales, probably wasn't going to have those forecasts on her desk Monday morning, when they were due.

Sure enough, he didn't. Pat reached for the phone, knowing that she was in the right.

"Alex, I don't have your forecasts."

"Oh, hey, Pat! How are you? Listen, things have been crazy here. We're working with a new system, and we have a bunch of guys who just came on. I've got so much paper on my desk, I guess it just slipped my mind. But I promise you, I'll get on it as soon as I can."

"But they were due by start of business today, and I need them."

"Pat, Pat. I know. We're all busy, but I'm not going to stop selling to do your paperwork. Just give me some time. I'll get it to you. Hey, Jim's here. Gotta go. You're the best. You're doin' a great job. See ya."

Pat felt completely frustrated. She didn't get closure, and so she couldn't do her job well. She calmed herself down, put on a pleasant face, and popped her head into Sam's office "just to say hello." Sam was the genial, avuncular CEO, who always had a smile and a glad hand for his senior staff. He loved delivering inspirational messages, but tended to surround himself with "yes people" and didn't really invite feedback that wasn't flattering.

Sam beamed and waved Pat in to sit down and have a Monday morning cup of coffee with him. She soon found herself "outflowing" about Alex and the frustration of working with people who couldn't be bothered to keep even the most minimal commitments. Sam commiserated, and even started telling her stories about other members of the executive committee who had done the same sort of thing with him. They agreed that it was tough and lonely at the top, but at least they could count on one another. Pat left feeling somewhat comforted by her deeper bond with Sam, but with no real constructive advice or action-oriented support.

An hour later, she found herself staring out the window, pondering her situation. It was true that Alex's first priority was selling, and that he was very busy. He had a whole different perspective, she knew, and that was understandable. After all, if he and his team didn't sell the product, none of them would have a job. But no amount of excusing his behavior, and no amount of understanding, made her feel any less frustrated.

Soon, she found herself making excuses not for Alex, but for herself. How could she be expected to do her job well if people didn't give her what she needed? And if the company itself didn't bother to enforce its rules with penalties, why should she even try? Wouldn't Alex be more likely to play by the rules if he had something to lose? Well, nobody appreciated what she and her people did, anyway. It wasn't sexy, finance. Of course, the company would go under if they stopped doing it, but nobody really understood how important it was. And if nobody saw that, why should they even try to hold the company together? It made sense just to do the minimum, to get by, and remember that if her forecasts were inaccurate or late, it was only because Alex's reports to her were inaccurate and late.

The problem was, none of this made Pat feel any better. And none of it made her more productive or more helpful to Bigger, Inc.

Meanwhile, Alex was no fool. He suspected Pat would be bad-mouthing him. Sure enough, he had lunch with Sheryl, the vice president for marketing, and, coincidentally, the person to whom Sam had confided his conversation with Pat. Sheryl tried to curry favor with Alex by "making sure he knew what was going on," but he was savvy enough to realize that, a few hours later, she would probably be making sure that Sam "knew what was going on" as well. So Alex just took in the information, and after lunch dropped by to see Ted, the human resources director.

Ted was actually in that day. Alex had noticed with amusement that Ted was something of a magician, with a disappearing act that few people noticed in the maelstrom of activity he created in his division. Actually, it was rather easy to disappear at Bigger, Inc.—either physically to the golf course or metaphorically into the staggering bureaucracy and avalanche of "to-do's." When Ted could be located, Alex found him to be a sympathetic listener. Ted shook his head and rolled his eyes when he heard about Pat's hard-boiled attitude and petty brownnosing. In fact, he recalled several instances in which Pat had done the same thing to him. And as a matter of fact, so had Randy, the bean-counting head of operations. And Sam could always be counted on to side with those kinds of people, Ted assured Alex.

"Them vs. Us" was up and running at Bigger, Inc., and began growing in magnitude and intensity with each day. Sam and Pat headed one small but powerful team. Alex and Ted headed the other side, which would make up in size what it lacked in institutional power. At this point, Sheryl was still able to run back and forth between the two sides, playing both for "Us" and for "Them." But not for long.

## The Consequences at Bigger, Inc.

How did this particular "Them vs. Us" dynamic affect the rest of the company, aside from its obvious consequences to morale and relationships?

When Pat couldn't make accurate and timely forecasts, everybody got stuck. The operations people didn't know how much product to make and couldn't control their inventory or distribution. If sales exceeded their forecast, then operations wouldn't have enough inventory and would be caught shorthanded. The engineers in operations focused on quality. If they got emergency orders because sales had underforecasted, they would be working until midnight for weeks on end, putting out what they consider to be a junk product because they were under the gun. Packaging was stuck as well, not knowing how much packaging to produce or when to produce it. Marketing couldn't put together their materials. Distribution couldn't make their plans, either.

Pinballing "Them vs. Us" dynamics began to emerge all over the company, with all of these divisions lining up against one another in various permutations: sales vs. marketing, packaging vs. distribution, operations vs. sales, etc.

And there was a squeeze play as well, as there almost always is when lack of closure precipitates this dynamic. Sales administration was a department that stood between sales and finance at Bigger, Inc. Their job was to take the rough figures that sales gave them and shape those figures in a way that would fit into Pat's system. Alex tried to blame them and get Pat focused on them instead of him. Pat found it easier to express her frustration to Jan, who headed up sales administration, than she did to Alex, so she started talking to Jan. But Jan couldn't do anything until she got the information from Alex, so sales administration got squeezed between the two sides.

The only people who consistently lined up together were Pat and Sam. Soon their collusion was so tight that two people were running Bigger, Inc., instead of the eight or nine people who had previously been running it. Sales declined and people began to leave. Those who stayed weren't as happy or productive as they had been. Word got around in the industry that Bigger was stagnant, and it was difficult to hire good people. The company began to lose the edge that it had once enjoyed.

## Startup, Inc.

Startup's issues were typical of those facing hot new companies. For the most part, they involved conflicts and lack of closure between sales/marketing and the engineers who designed and made the products. In Startup's case, those two positions were filled by the founders, Damon and Trevor.

Startup was under heavy pressure from investors to generate revenue. That was fine with Damon, the sales guy, because his people were compensated on the basis of how much they sold. Working on commission, he and his sales force were out there promising the world to potential customers. When they bothered to confer with Trevor, the lead designer, about when they needed the product, he told them, "That's unrealistic. We can't do that."

Like most sales managers at these companies, Damon turned a deaf ear to Trevor's warnings and continued to make promises on which he couldn't possibly deliver. Startup was faced with a dilemma that is often known as "the academic vs. the practical." Should you let your customers test the product and worry about the bugs only when the customer tells you about them (practical), or should you get the product perfect before it goes out the door (academic)? Obviously, Damon favored the practical and Trevor favored the academic.

Trevor and Damon reached a stalemate about the completion date for the product in question.

Trevor kept saying, "We can't do it."

Damon kept saying, "We have to do it."

Trevor didn't give Damon a genuine time when they *could* do it, and Damon didn't think to ask him for one. Their lack of closure was classic.

After a few of these "discussions," Trevor simply shut down and stopped talking. He was no longer willing to be the messenger of information that, however accurate, was not going to be given credence. He gave up and decided to let Damon hang himself.

Both Damon and Trevor were frustrated, and both started buzzing and gathering around them anyone in the small company who would listen—from the investors to the janitor.

## The Consequences at Startup, Inc.

"Them vs. Us" battle lines were clearly drawn, and it wasn't long before the rest of the company got involved. Damon won this battle, and they shipped the product with a lot of bugs.

That brought customer service into the picture. They were angry at both Damon and Trevor, because they spent all day listening to customers scream at them about the faulty product. Once Rayette, the head of customer service, found herself pushing back at a customer, "Look, it's not my fault. The designers put this thing together and sales rushed it out!"

Startup's credibility with customers took a further beating, and soon it didn't matter much *when* the product would be ready. Nobody was very interested.

We've seen the tip of the iceberg. In the next chapter, we will see a little more about "Them vs. Us" and its expanded form, "muck." We will take a look at the bigger picture, and you will start to understand how you can use the Trust Model to start reaping benefits.

# 4

# The Culture of Muck

WE'VE SEEN HOW lack of closure leads to "Them vs. Us" dynamics. When "Them vs. Us" is not faced directly and resolved in a culture of closure, commitment, and communication, it inevitably grows into something bigger. The organization becomes embroiled in a culture of **muck**.

Teamwork means relationships, and relationships sometimes involve experiencing discomfort. This discomfort can take the form of frustration, stress, confusion, uncertainty, misunderstanding, anxiety, worry, wondering, disagreement, irritation, distraction, suspicion, impatience, isolation, and other uncomfortable feelings. *Muck* is the word we use for all types of discomfort that arise in working relationships. It can be represented by a person, a certain issue or topic, a part of the company, a clique, or anything that makes us uncomfortable.

When there is a way to clear these negative feelings through closure and direct communication, the organization benefits. Not only is the muck resolved, but relationships are strengthened and information is gathered about problems underlying the muck. These problems can then be fixed and further muck minimized. When there is no clear way to deal with these uncomfortable feelings, however, the result is a miasma of negative emotions that keep people stuck, unproductive, and unhappy—and that keep all the problems firmly in place because they are buried under muck.

Like a shadow created by light, muck derives its vitality from team energy. Muck increases in proportion to the speed at which the organization is moving. The more the team tries to accomplish, the more the work level intensifies, and the more people care, the higher the level of muck. Muck level is an indicator of team energy; absence of muck means a flat line on the team heart monitor.

What separates great teams from average teams, leadership organizations from random organizations, is *how they deal with muck*. A leadership organization sees muck as an opportunity. It uses muck to understand what is going on in the company, to build relationships and productivity, to harvest the benefits of its diversity, and to grow into a stronger, more competitive entity.

Before you can start capitalizing on muck, however, you must see what it looks like in all its disguises.

## What Is Muck?

Muck is almost always the result of not keeping an agreement (false commitment), not reaching agreement in the first place (lack of closure), or not raising issues in a timely manner (indirect communication). The Trust Model provides specific tools for avoiding or resolving each of these situations. The process of resolving muck is more efficient when you understand what muck is and how it works.

Mucky situations have two parts: the uncomfortable feelings everyone is experiencing, and the objective problem that lies underneath the muck. Late delivery of a product leads to frustration, failure to meet quality standards creates disappointment, and unexplained firings lead to fear and mistrust. The objective cost can be measured in time, money, productivity, and/or quality. The subjective cost is measured in currency less tangible, but no less critical—in trust, confidence, enthusiasm, commitment, energy, and morale.

It is as if the team's emotional inner life mirrors its external circumstances. We can determine what is going on either by examining the objective state of the team's business or by looking in the mirror at its associated emotional state. This "bridge of understanding" runs between the outer and inner world, and you can travel in either direction to work on the problem. An effective leader knows that muck can be an early indicator of problems long before they become obvious, and can use solutions such as consistent closure to create clarity and inspire the team's morale and performance.

The goal is to deal effectively with the feeling of muck, so that you can start to work on the external, objective problem beneath it—the late deliveries, the failure to meet quality standards, the unexplained firings. What separates great teams from ordinary teams is how well they do this.

## Examples of Muck

The *Oxford English Dictionary* defines *muck* as "the dung of cattle (usually mixed with decomposing vegetable refuse) used for manure." The definition also includes "anything disgusting." In *Webster's*, it is defined as "an untidy or messy condition; a state of confusion, uncertainty, or disorganization; a fouled-up condition." You can use the Trust Model to turn this manure into fertilizer.

Here are some examples of muck:

• One week before the first shipment to customers, it is discovered that someone forgot to arrange for the product packaging to arrive in time. Now shipments will be delayed for several weeks in spite of a fully functioning, revenue-generating, completed product. The person who forgot feels guilty, and the operations people who got the product ready on time are angry. This is *coordination muck*.

• The president calls a meeting to discuss the lack of cooperation between marketing and other departments. As it happens, the vice president for marketing is out of town during that meeting. The president is irritated that the marketing guy is always out of town, and the marketing guy is furious that the president "went behind his back." This is *communication muck*.

• The vice president for business development signs a license that exceeds the limits of another technology license with a third party, thereby creating a breach of contract with an important supplier. The supplier learns of this from a press release and sues. Legal is frustrated that business development didn't coordinate with them, the CEO wants to fire the VP of business development, and business development feels defensive and isolated. This is *legal muck*.

• A private company runs out of money as the investor supply dries up due to deteriorating market conditions. Everybody feels frustrated and dejected. This is *financial muck*.

• Over time, employees come to believe that they own their jobs, their territories, and their roles in the company—as if these things were their personal possessions. Management would prefer that they approach their jobs with the attitude that they need to keep providing evidence of their productivity and value. Management is resentful, and employees feel either guilty or angry. This is *entitlement muck*.

• A young couple is strolling through a garden one evening when, acting upon the bad advice of a local snake (not an unfamiliar experience in business), they decide to take a bite out of a forbidden apple. Upon discovery, the Employer ejects them from the premises under the world's first employee relocation package. This is *Original Muck*.

## The Clues to Muck

How can you tell if your organization is involved in muck? First of all, you probably don't want to go to work in the morning. Relationships are sticky, motivations are unclear, communication is stifled, nobody really knows what's happening, and there are no universally accepted ways to resolve these conditions.

Some specific clues that muck is accumulating on a team are: tardiness, missed deadlines, coffee-room buzzing and gossip, closed-door meetings, stealing paper clips, long lunches, mysterious turnover, conversations suddenly halted in the hallway when someone comes along, poor production or quality, interdepartmental "Them vs. Us" wrangling, silent team meetings, sarcasm, cynicism, crisis motivation, too many meetings, too much reorganization, too many formal grievances, long personal phone calls, poor sales, blame, continuous cries for more compensation, territory and empire building, job insecurity, isolation, and cries of "That's not in my job description."

When these and other clues are not addressed and resolved, the result is poor service, waning motivation, more justification and suspicion, and more muck.

---

## FOLK THEOREM VIII.
*The greatest unnecessary loss of time and energy in business is associated with unresolved muck.*

---

# Knee-Jerk Reactions to Muck

Clues are a call to action. Leadership organizations lay out specific remedies for muck through their Trust Models, but teams in random organizations—which is to say, most teams—don't know what to do with muck. So they react instinctively, in ways that rarely get to the source of the problem. The four most common knee-jerk reactions to muck are:

1. **Retreat from the situation.** Run from the room, slam the door, quit the job, change the topic, start an argument, or get defensive. Better yet, just sit in the meeting and stop talking. When we retreat, we are trying to change the situation in order to get out of the muck.

The disadvantages of retreat are obvious. Neither the muck, nor the external problem that lies at its source, gets handled—so they both persist. Emotions become increasingly negative, and work becomes increasingly unproductive. Going to work becomes a less positive experience, and everyone gets involved in the downward emotional and productivity cycle.

Retreats often take the form of making "never again" decisions: "I'm never disagreeing with that person again. . . . I'll never offer a second opinion or volunteer my initiative again. . . . I'll never ask for or offer help again. . . . I'll never have breakfast at home again. . . . I'll never get married again. . . ."

Sometimes these "never again" experiences originate in early childhood. Perhaps we knocked over a vase and broke it. We admitted what we did, and got punished. Especially if the punishment was extreme in comparison with what we did (and children have an exquisitely fine-tuned sense of fairness), we were devastated. We attempted to make sense of the experience by drawing a conclusion about ourselves. We might have said, "I will never admit my mistakes again." Clearly, that was what got us into trouble, so we'll never do it again. We then bring that "never again" decision to work and refuse to admit mistakes to our teammates.

There are many ways to say "never again"—withdrawing emotionally, becoming angry, going silent, quitting the team or the company, and just going through the motions, to name a few—and many situations about which to say it. We might decide we will "never again" tell the truth, play hard, play fair, disagree, trust (men, women, authority, people), say "No," and so on.

"Never again" decisions can also stem from adult experiences. If we trusted someone in authority and we feel they have betrayed us, for example, we might decide "never again" to trust people in authority.

Whole organizations can make "never again" decisions. One manufacturing company had a division with a long tradition of disruptive changes in leadership. This instability coincided with a loss of market share. The team concluded that the leadership changes were responsible for market deterioration and that their markets would continue to deteriorate as long as the leadership kept changing. They converted two external conditions that may or may not have been connected—change in leadership and declining markets—into a firm decision that one condition was responsible for the other and that market decline was inevitable as long as the leadership kept changing. That "never again" decision had to be addressed directly before they could move forward.

"Never again" retreats are valiant efforts to avoid getting involved in the same kind of muck again, but they don't work. In fact, not handling muck ensures that it will resurface wherever you go—the new city, the new company, the new job, the new spouse and children, the new car, the new house. Wherever you try to retreat, the muck will follow.

**2. Avoid the problem—the person, issue, or conversation that stirs up muck for you.** There is a subtle distinction between this reaction and the retreat strategy, in which we actually encounter muck and then head for the hills. When we try to avoid muck, we either pretend it isn't there at all or we go out of our way not to run into it.

This requires that we invest substantial energy in knowing where the muck is and ascertaining the best routes around it. If I am avoiding Sally, for instance, I have to know where she is. That means I have to be thinking about her, on some level, all the time. Otherwise, how could I avoid her? Whenever we try to avoid a person, thought, challenge, controversy, or opinion, we must carry the associated muck around with us wherever we go. The drain on our energy is staggering—and the avoidance itself creates even *more* muck. Eventually, it becomes more uncomfortable to keep avoiding the muck, and thereby creating new muck, than it does to confront it. Trying to deny that the muck exists doesn't make us any more comfortable.

3. **Handle the muck, but not the problem itself.** This common pitfall occurs when we deal with the mucky feelings and heal the relationships among people, but don't take the next step and deal with the external condition beneath the muck. We might go for "good communication," for instance, without taking the next step and dealing with the lack of closure that gave rise to people's feelings that they weren't communicating with one another.

When we focus on "fixing the feelings," people go away feeling better *for a while*. But if we don't deal with the underlying problem, it hangs around. Before you know it, there is more muck. Sally and Tom no sooner handle their bad feelings than Sharon and Dave get caught in the same quagmire. Whatever gave rise to the trouble between Sally and Tom—it might have been an intrinsic flaw in the organizational structure, lack of closure, pretended commitments, consistently inaccurate sales projections, or a host of other problems—never got addressed. Over time, more and more people get less and less enjoyment from work until the original problem gets handled.

This happened at a church that ultimately had to call in a conflict-resolution team from the national organization to mediate a dispute between the minister and the board of directors. There had been conflicts over a proposed expansion and other financial matters, and feelings had grown quite heated. The conflict-resolution team came in and calmed everybody down temporarily. Board members and the minister got back on an even keel emotionally, and the muck appeared to be gone. But the fundamental issues of whether or not to expand and how to proceed financially were never handled, and so the muck took over again almost as soon as the conflict-resolution team walked out the door.

By the time muck has taken hold, there have probably been multiple failures to reach closure, false commitments, unclear communications, and/or external problems in the organization. Dealing only with the surface muck, without addressing these deeper issues, ensures that the muck will arise again. . . . and again and again.

4. **Dramatize the issue indirectly, rather than confront it head-on.** Sometimes we don't want to talk about muck, but we want to get rid of the discomfort—so we act out our difficulty and hope that somebody will notice, come to our rescue, and do something about it without our having to speak to it directly.

We use the "cough-drop example" to illustrate this dynamic. Say that Don is giving a speech and develops a cough. He wants a cough drop and thinks, "Gee, I could just ask if anyone has one." But before the words come out, a series of reservations rush through his mind. Would people think he wasn't being professional, showing up to speak without being prepared for needing a cough drop? He didn't see anyone in the audience sneezing or coughing, so they might not even *have* a cough drop.

Don's internal dialogue got worse and worse. He thought that if these people were actually listening to him, they would see him coughing and bring him a cough drop. They must not be listening. They must not care. So he coughed more, he coughed louder, he coughed more dramatically. Still, nothing happened. The people in the audience, who probably would have been delighted to get him a cough drop if he'd only asked for one, were mystified.

---

### FOLK THEOREM IX.
*You can ask for your cough drop, or you can go on hacking.*

---

This dynamic took hold in one division that was headed by an imperious manager who never wanted his staff to get credit for anything. He believed that the way to keep people productive was to keep them lean and hungry, so he rarely gave promotions or raises. People in his division didn't want to speak directly to the issue because they were afraid of him, so they convinced disgruntled people in other divisions to join them in an assault on top management's "unfair salary policies"—diverting the attention from the imperious manager to *his* bosses, dramatizing their issue without speaking to it directly and hoping that the top bosses would figure out what was going on.

## The Effect of Muck on Trust

Muck and trust are incompatible. They cannot coexist. The mind cannot simultaneously experience the discomfort of muck *and* the emotional expectation of trust. And when muck and trust contend on the emotional level, muck always wins.

Angie's boss came down on her hard when he didn't like the part of the annual report that she'd prepared. He raised his voice and said the report "needs a lot of work," but didn't say what kind of work. She was stung. Angie knew intellectually that this was a good company, that she had a bright future in it, that her boss's behavior that day was the exception rather than the rule, and that he would probably recognize that he had acted inappropriately and apologize within twenty-four hours—but while she was still in the muck of her hurt feelings, there was no way she could experience trust. All she wanted in that moment was to quit and go work for the competition.

It's not possible for us to say to ourselves, "Well, I'm in the muck right now, but it will soon pass and everything will go back to normal." The psyche is not so easily fooled. Viewed from within, muck appears unlimited. A genuine experience of muck, an experience that has the possibility of actually leading somewhere new, feels as though you are sunk in its depths. The best thing you can do while having a full-blown muck experience is simply to think of the muck as an intellectual concept. You then proceed to resolve the muck, not expecting to *feel* better until that process is complete.

---

### FOLK THEOREM X.
*It is impossible to trust fully when you are in muck.*

---

## Muck as Fertilizer

Muck is a natural human condition. It's what we do with muck that separates leadership organizations from random organizations, successful enterprises from unsuccessful.

When you understand muck, you can mine it for gold. When you dig into hallway buzz, for instance, you may find a perception of favoritism toward one department that needs to be addressed openly and frankly. When you get to the bottom of your partner's hesitancy about a certain program, you may discover that your innate optimism is driving him nuts, and that he would like a bit more groundedness in your conversations. When you dig into what is behind the grumbling over revenue forecasts, you may discover that some members of the sales team simply don't know what they're doing, but are open to support from others.

Most people make some effort to deal with muck when they encounter it, but most of these attempts are ineffective because they don't clearly understand the dynamics at work and don't have access to the Trust Model. Unless we deal with muck in the context of a conscious, proven process like the Trust Model, we run the risk of actually making it worse. Unless there is a universally accepted, standard practice for dealing with muck, we usually get our own agendas and our old habits tangled up with the team problem, resulting in even more muck.

---

## FOLK THEOREM XI.
*Decisions made while you are still in muck lead to*
*new muck.*

---

Under these conditions, muck resurfaces again and again, sometimes as merely a low-grade distraction, but sometimes flaring into an enormous frustration. Not only that, but muck doesn't get any better if we just let it alone. Either we're making it worse by trying to treat the muck while we're still in it, or we ignore it, deny it, or throw up our hands and do nothing. If we do the latter, we soon realize that, left untreated, muck continues to grow.

---

## FOLK THEOREM XII.
*Untreated muck grows.*

---

So what do we do? How do we go about using muck as fertilizer? First, we don't blame ourselves or others for getting into the muck. Everybody gets into muck; that's not the problem. It is not "wrong" to experience muck, and it does not indicate weakness or failure. In fact, the level of muck in an organization is a good indicator of its vitality, its energy, its commitment, and how fast it is moving. Absence of muck means an organizational flat line.

The best approach to muck is to look it in the eye, ask what it has to teach us, and deal with it directly using trust principles. *Going through muck can be done in minutes.* The great time-consumer is *not* going through it—holding on to it, retreating from it, avoiding it, pretending it isn't there, playing with it, or giving it undue importance. Once we have worked through the muck in one situation, it becomes much easier to work through it in the next.

Dealing with muck simply involves gaining closure. Closure eliminates the discomfort associated with muck, restores trust, and opens the way to effective action. Whether the muck arose out of not keeping an agreement (false commitment), not reaching agreement in the first place (closure), or not raising issues in a timely manner (direct communication), the Trust Model provides a solution. It encourages behavior that avoids muck in the first place, and it provides clear remedies to resolve muck when it does appear.

As you clear up muck, you can discover the problems beneath it— problems that you might find in no other way.

---

### FOLK THEOREM XIII.

*Your next great business strategy—your turnaround program or your much needed market innovation—is lying there in the muck, waiting to be discovered.*

---

Let's look at how our two fictional companies, Startup, Inc., and Bigger, Inc., became embroiled in the culture of muck.

## Startup, Inc.

After operating out of a garage for two years, Startup's founders, Damon and Trevor, finally attracted some venture capital. One condition of the investment was that the two founders hire a CEO experienced in building strong, high-growth companies. Eager to escape their undercapitalized state, Damon and Trevor quickly complied. They recruited a professional leader with clearly defined responsibilities and the usual financial incentives. They were on the map at last; they were *real*.

But in about a week, Trevor started acting weird. He'd always had a reputation for being superpunctual, but now he started showing up late for meetings. He would "forget" details of agreements he'd made just the day before. He began speaking negatively about other members of the team. Finally, he gave two very different stories to the media about the direction that Startup was taking, and this prompted a flurry of concerned calls from customers and other potential investors. Damon was appalled.

As is often the case with startups that become successful, Damon and Trevor had inadvertently stumbled into a good decision. In this case, it was the hiring of Randy, the new CEO. Randy had prior experience in building trust-based teams and understood the underlying principles very well.

Rather than reacting negatively to Trevor, Randy saw this particular piece of muck as an opportunity. Instead of punishing Trevor or trying to undermine or overpower him, Randy started looking for what might be behind his behavior. Through a series of one-on-ones and facilitated meetings with Trevor and other leaders in the company, he found it. Trevor had unconscious, unspoken fears that he would have to compromise some dearly held values in the "cold world of business" on the way to the "big time." These fears had led to unconscious misgivings about the growth that would come with the venture investment, and a weak commitment to expanding the business.

Randy's early discovery resulted in a clear agreement that protected Trevor's values while meeting the business requirements of the company. Startup not only survived to obtain additional funding, but has gone on to create an excellent position in the market.

## Bigger, Inc.

Bigger's muck epiphany originated with Jan, the head of sales administration, who got caught in the squeeze play between CFO Pat and Alex, the vice president of sales. When Jan figured out what was happening—and it didn't take her long—she was furious. She knew it took a lot to get CEO Sam's attention, and so she started talking with the competition about a position, and even floated her resume with a few other companies.

That got Sam's attention, and he brought in a team trained in trust principles to start weeding through the muck. They talked to many people in different settings and got to the bottom of the problem. It soon became clear that Alex didn't want to take the time away from selling to do forecasting, and that he was terrified of not finding the balance between giving Pat reasonable, believable projections (that might result in escalating quotas) and not overprojecting so that he and his team would look bad if they didn't make the targets. When he had a chance to air these concerns to Pat and Sam, who had received a crash course in listening from the facilitator, they found they could work together to come up with honest, doable figures.

Using trust principles, they were able to deal with both the muck and the underlying objective problem.

In the next chapter, we explore the inner workings of closure and commitment, your two most powerful tools for building a trust-based leadership organization.

# Part III

# THE SOLUTION

# 5

# Communicating for Closure and Commitment

CLOSURE AND COMMITMENT are your two most powerful tools for building a trust-based leadership organization, and they both rely heavily on good communication. When you have these two powerful principles in place, the rest follows easily. You can cut quickly and consciously through "Them vs. Us," muck, and other problems that undermine random organizations.

Closure and commitment are learned skills. You can master them yourself, and then pass them on to your team or your organization using the step-by-step program outlined in Part IV.

In this chapter, we'll look at the best ways to communicate for closure and commitment.

## What Is Closure?

Remember, closure means that every interaction ends with a promise that includes time. In other words, who will do what, and by when. It is the difference between saying "I'll get to that" (nonclosure) and saying "I'll let you know what the sales forecast is by close of business Thursday." The latter statement makes it clear what will happen, by when. It eliminates wondering and worrying, and gives a way to measure whether or not I've done what I said I would do.

Here's the tricky part. Not everybody volunteers of their own accord to get you the sales forecast by close of business Thursday. Sometimes you need to *bring* the conversation to that kind of closure. It might happen like this. I ask Alice if she can meet in my office at 9:00 on Tuesday morning. If she says "Yes," then we have closure. If she says "No," we also have closure on the question of meeting at 9:00 Tuesday morning. We're not going to do it. I can stop investing energy in that particular date and time, and can move on to inquire about another time and date. I may ask her if she can meet Wednesday at 10:00. Again, she says "Yes" or "No." When we find a mutually agreeable time, then we will have closure on the subject of when we will meet.

But if Alice says, "I don't know, I'll get back to you," then we do not have closure. This is the most likely response in a random organization. To move toward closure, I might say, "Can you give me a time by when you'll get back to me?"

In a random organization that does not value closure, Alice might say, "No, I can't give you a time. I have to check with Jim and Ted, and we have our own problems."

If I truly want closure, I have to take another step. I want to get from Alice a time by which she can give me a time. I might say something like, "Alice, I understand that you have to check with Jim and Ted, but your input is important to me and I want to make sure our meeting happens. Can you give me a time when you'll be able to give me a time?"

These kinds of communications can require some skill and practice. That's why whenever we teach closure in an organization, we also teach the communication skills to stay connected with people while you are in the process of reaching closure. Teaching those skills and establishing a culture in which everyone is committed to closure are the cornerstones of a leadership organization. Without those skills, we are asking the person who is trying to reach closure to endure very high levels of discomfort.

Being willing to keep going, even when Alice tries to put me off, tells her that I care about what we're doing together. If I didn't care, I'd just let it go. I wouldn't press for the meeting with her. If I didn't support her in reaching closure with me, it would suggest that Alice wasn't really that important and that what we were doing together didn't really matter to me.

---

### FOLK THEOREM XIV.
*Leaving things open, without closure, usually means they do not get done.*

---

Part of communicating to reach closure consistently is understanding how to craft a good *cycle of closure*.

## Crafting the Cycle of Closure

Closure happens in cycles. A cycle is a full circuit. There are many kinds of cycles: communication cycles, sales cycles, research and development cycles, production cycles, marketing cycles, packaging and distributing cycles, and so on.

Each cycle has four parts: *a beginning, an activity, an end,* and *an investment.* The first three are *external.* The first three parts of a production cycle, for instance, might be the idea and planning for a new product, the actual making of it, and sending it out into the market. The fourth part of the cycle, the investment, is an *internal* component of closure. It is the emotional investment or commitment of everyone involved in the project. Human emotion powers business cycles. We have to care about a cycle in order to continue it. To the extent that the people involved in the production cycle care about it, it will succeed.

Cycles can be large or small. The cycle for a new product is large, but a cycle might be as small as lunch with a coworker. The invitation would be the beginning, eating lunch together would be the activity, and the end would come when you pay the bill and leave the restaurant. The investment in the lunch cycle could be large or small, depending on the feelings and purposes of the people involved.

Even a conversation can be a cycle. I ask Joe if he will come fix my computer this afternoon. He says "Yes." I ask him what time he will be there, and he says 3:00. I thank him. That small conversational cycle has closure. The larger cycle of him actually fixing my computer will reach closure when he shows up at 3:00 and fixes it.

Closure occurs at the end of a cycle. At the end of each cycle, you assess whether or not the goal was achieved. This means that each cycle is an opportunity to win or lose, and then play the game again.

Without every element of the cycle—beginning, activity, end, and investment—you cannot win.

In our example from Chapter 2 about asking Henry to get a ham sandwich, the beginning of the cycle would be the request for a sandwich. Because Henry leaves the room without replying, we don't know whether or not he has agreed to get the sandwich, and so the cycle isn't complete. There is no closure. We have no idea whether or not he intends to get the sandwich—and if he intends to get it, whether he will do so in fifteen minutes or next week.

The emotional signal that a cycle is not complete is that we start wondering. We don't know what is happening, and wondering about it takes our energy away from other tasks. The emotional investment in the ham sandwich may be small—but when a promotion or some other issue with a higher emotional investment is at stake, that wondering quickly turns to *worry*.

When we don't get closure, it sometimes involves an error in setting up the cycle. Errors in setting up the first three elements of the cycle are usually mechanical. They include uncoordinated starts, inadequate communication of the vision, insufficient resources, an unrealistic time frame, goals with fuzzy or unrecognizable benchmarks, frequently or unconsciously changing goals, and lack of a defined end point.

Errors of emotion or investment, the fourth element in the cycle, occur when the head is nodding but the heart isn't in it. In these cases, we are almost always heading for a false, or pretended, commitment. Not ensuring the investment is the most common cause of nonclosure. When people aren't truly committed, then deadlines will be missed, quality will suffer, and promises won't be kept. When the emotional investment is truly in place, these mechanical errors are easily avoided.

Complete closure means the completion of a cycle, but this is not always possible immediately. My conversation with Alice about when we would meet, for instance, could not come to complete closure until she had talked to Jim and Ted. In these cases, the next best thing is intermediate closure. That's what I was going for with my follow-up questions. Getting intermediate closure is an art—one that is well worth mastering.

## The Next Best Step: Intermediate Closure

Intermediate closure means getting "a time for a time," or a time by which the other person can get back to you about when they can get back to you. Intermediate closure requires communication that is clear but at the same time connected, tactful, and respectful.

With intermediate closure, everybody still knows who is going to do what, by when—but the cycle is smaller. You're not completing the cycle of setting a time for the meeting, for instance; you're just completing the cycle of setting a time when you can set a time.

Nevertheless, getting intermediate closure is crucial in those cases where you can't get complete closure immediately. It maintains the integrity of a culture of closure and trust, and gets everybody in the habit of closing cycles—even if those cycles have to be shortened in order to be closed. No one has to waste time wondering and worrying, and so time, productivity, and energy are saved. If Alice can get back to me by noon on Friday about when she can meet, I don't have to waste any more energy on that subject. I'm on hold until noon on Friday, but I know that I'll get a time and date for our meeting then.

The ability to gain intermediate closure is especially important when you are still in the process of building a culture of closure. People may not be in the habit of thinking ahead enough to close larger cycles, but you can always reach some form of intermediate closure. If Hank goes to his boss and asks for new computer equipment so that he can do his job better, he may get a "Yes" with a date attached. Or he may get a "No." In the case of either "Yes" with a date or "No," Hank has closure. He may prefer the "Yes," but even with a "No" he has discovered "gravity," the truth for now. He may be disappointed, but getting a clear "No" is better than hanging out in limbo. He knows it's not possible to get the equipment by going to his boss, so he can either reconcile himself to the situation and plan around it, or he can think of alternative ways to get the equipment.

The third possibility, "Maybe," is Hank's opportunity to hone his intermediate closure skills. The "Maybe" may take the form of "I'll get back to you," "I'll put in for it in the budget," "I'll check around and see," or some other answer that leaves Hank dangling.

At that moment, Hank can move toward intermediate closure with some form of "Thanks. When can you get back to me on that?"

Suppose the boss says, "How should I know? I just told you I have to consult the powers that be. I don't know when I'm going to hear."

This conversation wouldn't happen in a leadership organization, in which closure has the highest priority and people who insist on it earn the highest respect. But in organizations that are making the transition to being leadership organizations, someone has to be the first to break the closure barrier. If that person were Hank, he might say, "I see. Can you tell me when you might know when you would know?" Again, the message this question conveys is that Hank cares. In a way that genuinely honors his boss, he is saying, "I'm not going to go away, because this is important to me."

If Hank doesn't pursue closure, if he just walks away with a "Maybe," then he has communicated that the boss's answer was good enough and that he, Hank, doesn't care very much. He is walking away into the limbo of wondering and worrying, because in fact he *does* care, in spite of what he has inadvertently communicated. The ambiguity of nonclosure leads to frustration and blame, which can be used to "justify" lower performance. Eventually, Hank may come to feel, "If the boss doesn't care, why should I?"

## Common Obstacles to Closure

Most people see the benefits of closure immediately, and their responses range from relief to enthusiasm. But it's good to remember as you communicate with people that we all have certain obstacles to closure. The most common obstacles are behaviors and personal styles that invite distrust and defensiveness. Some of these are:

- hidden agendas, either personal or departmental
- lack of ability to tell the truth
- gossiping and talking behind people's backs
- "Them vs. Us" mentality, either personal or departmental
- poor downward communication
- interdepartmental conflict (blaming, finger pointing, etc.)
- insufficient emotional attachment to the vision
- procrastination
- being rigid or demanding
- avoiding conflict
- denying that there is a problem

## It's Just a Habit

Why don't we close cycles and interactions? It's not that people don't care, though we sometimes *communicate* that we don't care. And it's not that people aren't capable. We find that, almost without exception, nonclosure is simply a *habit*. Again, be compassionate in your communication. Remember that we are all creatures of habit and need to be moved gently up to the next level of functioning.

In fact, nonclosure is actually multiple habits. It's my habit, working with your habit, working with everyone else's habit. If Hank doesn't pursue the computer equipment question with his boss, it's probably because he doesn't have the habit of reaching closure. If the boss doesn't volunteer closure, doesn't follow Hank's lead when he asks questions that ask for closure, or doesn't actually guide the conversation to closure when he notices that Hank isn't doing so, it's just because the boss doesn't have the habit of reaching closure either.

If either person involved in the interaction changes his or her habit, the level of closure goes up. If I become more used to getting closure than not getting it, I will be more likely to ask Alice the uncomfortable questions I need to ask in order to reach closure about our meeting. If she becomes more used to getting closure than not getting it, she will be more likely to volunteer closure without my having to ask. If we *both* change our habits and get more used to closure than nonclosure, the level of closure goes up exponentially. We then have a fail-safe system. If I don't create the closure, she will. If she doesn't, I will. And we will both support the other in creating the closure, because we realize the benefits.

If an organization has learned to value closure, if everyone in that organization knows what needs to happen in order to create win-win closure in every interaction, and if they have been given the skills to do so even in tough situations, then you have a workplace where closure is almost guaranteed. You have three backups: one person, the other person, and the organization. Buzzing and "Them vs. Us" behavior become the glaring exceptions.

## The Two-Way Street

As with all communication, closure communication is a two-way street.

Terry was the vice president of engineering at a software company. One morning Ned, the sales manager, called to ask her when the 2.0 version of their product would be ready to ship. She had no idea, she said, because she was working with some new programmers. She didn't know how long the development would take them or when they would be willing to give a completion date.

Ned knew that his question had put Terry on the spot, and that she had responded with some natural defensiveness. He also realized that closure was a new concept at their company, and that they were going to have to support one another in order to make it work. He recognized the habit of nonclosure not only in Terry, but in himself as he contemplated asking the next uncomfortable question. He didn't really want to press her, but he knew they would both win in the long run if he did.

Ned took a deep breath and asked, "Is there a time by which you could give me a completion date, Terry?" That request depended only on her ability to size up the programmers. That was somewhat within her control, and Ned's supportive and respectful way of asking the question helped. Terry was able to give him a date by which she agreed to have assessed the programmers' ability and spoken with them about a final date. Because Ned was persistent in supporting closure, her "No" to the first question didn't stop the process or send the organization down an unproductive "Them vs. Us" path.

In a leadership organization, both people in the interaction are responsible for creating the closure. Ned and Terry's situation could have worked the other way. When Terry initially told Ned she couldn't come up with a shipping date, he might have let it go and walked away from the situation. If he had done that, it would have been up to her to recognize her own habit of nonclosure and do something about it. She might have called him back and said, "Look, Ned, I can't give you a shipping date right away because I don't know how fast my new programmers can work or what their assessment of the situation is. But I should have that information in a month. Let me work with them for awhile, talk to them about the project, and get back to you with an authentic shipping date by May 1."

In a leadership organization, people know how critical it is to close every interaction and they have the skills to do so. That's what creates the competitive edge. Your competitors will copy your technology, and they may even beat it. They may steal your people. But they cannot copy a team that is so connected, that has such trust, that it closes interactions on a regular basis. That is a unique culture, and you can build it in your organization. When new people begin working for you, it doesn't take eight quarters to build up trust. They are simply enveloped in the culture of trust, and they catch on quickly.

## Communication Skills for Closure

When an organization first starts working with closure, muck has often accumulated between individuals, between job functions, between layers of management, and between different geographical locations—all due to lack of closure. In medical insurance, they call this a "preexisting condition," and it is considered potentially costly. Just as your insurance company often won't reimburse you for preexisting conditions, you can't create closure until you first deal with unresolved muck. The following sections describe some of the most valuable communication skills for moving toward closure and commitment.

### Prevailing and Understanding Conversations

Prevailing conversations are those in which we want our point of view to prevail over other points of view. We want to prove that we are smarter, righter, more persuasive, experienced, charming, or articulate than the person to whom we are speaking.

Understanding conversations are those in which we want to be understood but also to understand why others see what they see. We get behind the other person's eyes and appreciate their perspective as well as our own. The point of an understanding conversation is to make and keep a connection with the other person, while understanding both the information and emotional content of what he or she is saying. The Greek root of *understanding* means to look at an issue from so many points of view that you can even "stand under" it before selecting the perspective from which you will act. When you use understanding conversations to arrive at decisions, you can select from among the best of five, ten, twenty, or more points of view, rather than from only one or two.

We are trained almost from preschool to have prevailing conversations. In leadership organizations, we retrain ourselves to have understanding conversations. We begin to enjoy the benefits of seeing things the way others do, and using all those points of view to gain a higher order of intelligence with which to make good decisions and find solutions.

Intelligence is the ability to look at a problem from many different angles *before* you select the one to which you will devote your resources. It's like making a change on the blueprint rather than waiting until the whole structure is built and having to knock out a wall. It's a lot easier, a lot less expensive, and it develops courage.

## Assumptive and Nonassumptive Questions

In understanding conversations, we distinguish between assumptive and nonassumptive questions. Assumptive questions contain an assumption—of the right answer, of what is accurate information, of the listener's response to what is being said, of something. These questions often leave the listener feeling intruded upon.

Nonassumptive questions focus on the objective reality of the situation, not on judging the subjective qualities of the people involved or making assumptions about what is going on. They also invite the person being questioned to stand back from the situation and look at it from some distance to gain objectivity.

For example, an assumptive question to someone who shows up after the start of a meeting might be, "Why are you always late?" A nonassumptive question might be, "What happened?" If a project isn't completed on time, the assumptive question might be, "Why can't you get this done?" The nonassumptive question might be, "What happened with our project schedule?" "Why are you bored?" is an assumptive question. "How are you doing?" is a nonassumptive question. "Still behind?" is an assumptive question. "How are we doing with our timeline?" is a nonassumptive question.

Asking nonassumptive questions shows respect for the other person, just as assumptive questions show lack of respect and a desire to impose our own agenda.

## Staying Connected

Understanding conversations allow for give-and-take. They also require that, even in the midst of this give-and-take, we stay connected with one another. Staying connected means that we do more than listen to the facts and circumstances being discussed. It goes beneath these surface matters and engages deeper emotional levels. It says to the other person that, even if we disagree, we value him or her as a human being.

Keeping connected with the other person, regardless of the content of the conversation, can be one of the most challenging aspects of listening. This skill starts with genuinely caring about what the other person says, without seeking either to fix the situation or to discard or discount it. Nothing shuts down a connection faster than dismissing the other person's point of view. When a conversation is emotionally heated, sometimes it's best to take a break and set a time to resume. Let the fire burn itself out a little so that you can both approach the subject in a cooler state of mind later.

## Tact and Respect

Maintaining this connection requires tact and respect. Tact doesn't mean we are so polite that we never get to the point. It does mean that we treat people as valued human beings, whether or not we agree with them. Merely being polite, without getting to the point, may make for an emotionally gentle communication—but one that doesn't reach real closure. And while tact also includes accuracy, accuracy alone is not enough. "That is a bad idea" may be a completely accurate statement, but the proud owner of the idea probably feels uncomfortable and not very connected to the speaker.

When you're enmeshed in discomfort, it can be challenging to communicate with tact and respect. You may still have a win-lose attitude toward the person or situation that made you uncomfortable. One way to move toward closure under these circumstances is to look and see how you may have participated in the situation. When you have seen your part in the matter, you create a different atmosphere between you and the other party. It's easier to communicate with tact and respect through an understanding conversation. If you can also admit your mistakes and say how you intend to change your approach, you show how willing you are to reach closure. It becomes easier for everyone to move forward and share the success.

Suppose you've had a few unpleasant encounters with George over the Smith account. If you want to begin again, with communication that moves toward closure and a win-win outcome, you might say something like, "George, I'd like to get some time with you to talk over the Smith account. Would you take a few minutes to hear me out, and also to go over your views again? I want to make sure I understand what you're suggesting, so that we can get over the impasse and make this work for everyone." This approach is far more effective than, "George, we have to get to the bottom of this Smith thing."

## Being Nonjudgmental

This means separating the act of receiving information from the act of judging it. For a good outcome, we must both receive information and judge it. But these two functions must be kept separate from one another until the communication is complete. If we judge the information before the sender finishes giving it to us, he or she will hesitate to give us any further information that he or she believes we are judging negatively. The sender may even change the information as he or she delivers it, depending on how he or she believes we are judging it.

More importantly, receiving the full communication before we respond or judge is a way of honoring the communicator. It says that our connection in this moment is more important than being right or wrong, smart or dumb, happy or upset.

For some people, listening without judging is a new mode of communication. It may feel passive at first, but it rises to a high art when you learn to include in your listening not just the content of the message, but also the feeling tone and emotional subtext of what is being said—and perhaps as important, what is *not* being said. In its most effective form, nonjudgmental listening completely re-creates the other person's point of view within ourselves.

## Good Listening

Suppose the other person says something with which you don't agree. Do you interrupt? Probably not, if you are having an understanding conversation. You might occasionally interrupt to clarify what the other person said—using nonassumptive questions, not questions that might invite a defensive response—but it's best to keep these interruptions to a minimum.

When Tom's daughter, Anna, reached adolescence, she seemed to be the same wonderful person she had always been, but a bit more complex. So Tom invited her out to lunch and suggested that she just talk. He promised not to interrupt. She was skeptical at first, but she agreed to talk and let him listen. She started out tentatively, but slowly built in intensity until all the big issues emerged: boyfriends, girlfriends, school, brother, Mom, hair, clothes, and urban blight. Tom sat for over an hour without saying a word. By the end of their "talk," Anna was exuberant.

"Dad, that was the best conversation we have ever had!" she said.

This event occurred about fifteen years ago, and set the pattern for their communication to this day. Anna would be invited to say whatever was on her mind, and Tom would listen—interested but detached, withholding judgment, and connected. Anna would talk about certain issues, emotions would peak, and the conversation would move over the crest and down the other side of the hill. Then the two of them would pick up topics one by one, work them through together, look for new possibilities, and engage in traditional problem-solving.

These conversations worked not because of Tom's abundant supply of readily available solutions—all dads have that—but because Anna felt respected. She sensed that the connection between them was more important to Tom than the outcome of any particular issue, and she was right. In the same way, team members feel respected and trusted when the connection is clearly more important that the information being received or the decisions being made.

## Confirmation

Let people know that you've heard and understood what they said. You might repeat the information back to them, nod, or actually tell them that you've understood. Of course, they will only know that they were truly understood if your actions are consistent with that understanding.

## Focus Toward Closure

As you are listening and understanding, being open to the other person and what he or she says, and practicing all the communications skills we've just described, remember to keep focusing toward closure. You are involved in more than a friendly chat that makes both of you feel good. Your purpose is to reach closure, to bring the conversation around to who will do what, and by when. Without this element, it doesn't matter how good both of you feel *during* the conversation. The negative dynamics that arise out of nonclosure will follow quickly unless you close the issue you are discussing.

## Acknowledgment of Closure (Preferably in Writing)

It's important to acknowledge that you have reached closure. This might be saying, "Then I'll meet you in my office at 9:00 Tuesday morning to discuss the Smith deal." It might be, "So my understanding of what you've just said is that you won't consider giving me a raise until next July." Or, "Then we'll go ahead with the deal, starting February 1."

Obviously, not every closure needs to be put into writing—but even in the case of confirming a meeting time, it's best if everybody at least writes it down in his or her calendar. In closure, it's better to err on the side of writing than nonwriting.

## Soliciting People's Willingness

The principle of soliciting willingness is a powerful way to create emotional connection so that you can move on to the issues at hand. When we don't bother with the emotional part of a communication, we don't usually get far. Establish the human connection with the other person before you tackle the issues. "Larry, we need to talk" may be accurate and to the point, but it does not establish much of a connection or solicit Larry's willingness. In fact, it presumes that you are in charge and Larry had better knuckle under. It's a communication that is likely to invite resentment and fear. You will probably get a better reaction with, "Larry, I'd like to discuss the sales forecast. Would you be willing to take a few minutes to meet?"

You have told Larry what you want and solicited his willingness. Furthermore, if he indicates that he really does not want to talk about the sales forecast in spite of your tactful approach, you have probably learned something valuable about him.

Suppose you are sitting in a meeting, and a very quiet person starts to talk. The "small voice" is emerging. You want to encourage him, but it soon becomes apparent that he has gone off track. You don't want to be insensitive, but you need to bring the conversation back to the topic at hand. Everyone is watching to see what you do.

The first step is to acknowledge his contribution. You might say, "Thanks for speaking up on this subject." Then ask clearly for what you want, and solicit his willingness to support you in achieving it. "We want to hear from everybody, and we also need to be brief. Can you help by addressing the issue directly?" This creates a bridge back to the original topic.

Soliciting willingness can change the whole dynamic of a conversation. It puts control into other people's hands, and that makes them feel more comfortable. They can then take the next step and, since they feel acknowledged both intellectually and emotionally, they are probably more disposed to move toward closure.

Remember that when you acknowledge someone, your acknowledgment needs to be authentic. In the example just given, the quiet person was willing to speak up—even if what he said was not to the point. That willingness alone is worth acknowledging. Phony or exaggerated acknowledgments are always seen as exactly what they are. They only make us seem manipulative and dilute the effect of our praise. The same principle applies to thanking someone for something you don't really want. You're likely to get more of the same.

These are some of the communications skills that help you move toward closure, rather than away from it. The goal in any leadership organization is to close 100 percent of all interactions. To do that, your people need not only motivation, but skills. When they acquire these things, that's when change can begin.

## Reaching Closure in Meetings

Meetings are the most expensive team activity, and therefore need to be the most productive. Meetings are also the single event where the interior experience of the connected team is at the same time expressed by its exterior physical configuration. Here is where inner and outer life synchronize, and meetings are therefore the most intense experience of team life. It is critical that the conduct of meetings be fully in line with the trust principles embraced by the team.

If meetings are the greatest opportunity to harvest the promise of the Trust Model, they can also be the clearest dramatization of its absence. In random organizations, meetings can be arenas for grudges, "Them vs. Us" dynamics, malicious obedience, silent resentment, unspoken fears, pretended commitments, filibustering, posturing to the boss, harsh judgment, public humiliation, win-lose competition, entrapment in limiting beliefs, and chronic and habitual nonclosure. People often focus on obstacles instead of what they can do.

The principles of closure described earlier, and the communication skills to make them work, provide a complete foundation for effective meetings. The speed, efficiency, and creativity of a team meeting will increase in proportion to the team's mastery of these skills.

The focus of every meeting should be on gaining closure. In fact, meetings drag on precisely when closure is not happening. Closure can be greatly facilitated by the way the meeting is organized and managed, and by the collective skills and intent of the participants. There are many good meeting primers in bookstores, and we will not attempt our own version here. Rather, our focus is on linking meeting protocol back to the underlying principles of the Trust Model.

The first concern, which is often missed, is the purpose of the meeting. Getting clear on the purpose of the meeting is an invitation to obtaining real buy-in and commitment. So the first question is: "Do we need to have this meeting?" One of the most dramatic results in organizations that move in the direction of trust and closure is fewer meetings, or shorter and more enjoyable meetings, as the air is cleared of fog and old habits. The purpose statement of a meeting could include information dissemination (large groups), brainstorming (small to medium groups), getting buy-in (small, focuslike groups), and decision-making.

Next is the agenda. The agenda is a statement of commitment to what must be closed. In order for people to commit to the meeting, you need to give them a chance to consider fully what they are buying into. This means that the agenda should be distributed before the meeting to let people see what will be discussed, prepare to discuss it, and if necessary, respond with suggested modifications to the topics. To avoid "Them vs. Us" dynamics with the meeting designers, it is useful to give all team members a chance to add their own proposals for topics. Agendas may also include time allotments for each topic.

Next is the meeting itself. The facilitator, who need not always be the most senior person, manages the meeting for closure. He or she keeps cycles separate, creates balanced air time, monitors communication for understanding vs. prevailing conversations, and seeks willingness to move forward. Some optional roles at meetings are: timekeeper (for highly organized agendas) and closer (the person dedicated to preventing time overruns and pretended closure).

Every meeting worth having should generate a document to support closure and create continuity. This document may include conclusions, who drew what assignments, what preparation is required for the next meeting, the next meeting's agenda, and how to give input into this next agenda. Hence, the scribe plays a key role. It is also a difficult role, so the team needs to support the scribe in verifying what has been said and decided after each section of the meeting. Leaving the scribe to figure this out after the meeting invites muck and creates delay.

The value of putting things in writing also extends to meeting preparation. It is very useful for people to bring their proposals in writing, especially when the team is going through the seven-step closure process (described in Chapter 6). This also reduces the length of the meeting, since these documents can be prepared and even distributed before people actually sit down together.

Handling slippage is an inevitable component of most meetings. The Trust Model allows for slippage to be handled publicly and immediately without humiliation. Tact and respect, judging the problem and not the person, and always moving toward closure are essential skills for maintaining people's dignity if their tasks have slipped. Give the person responsible for the slippage the first shot at proposing a solution. This reinforces his or her value rather than degrading it. Meetings conducted in this way become opportunities for constructive performance audits, as well as for recognition.

Let's look now at communicating for another powerful tool, commitment. Again, reviewing the principles of this tool gives us a sense of how best to communicate about it.

## What Is Commitment?

As we have said, commitment is a condition of no conditions, a promise with no hidden "if's" attached to it. It is not an unconditional guarantee that you will produce exactly the results you promised. Life intercedes too often to make such a simpleminded assurance. A commitment is not an unconditional guarantee of outcome, but an unconditional promise that you intend to do what you say you will do.

A commitment doesn't mean, for instance, "I'll show up at 8:00 if the traffic is okay." It means, "I'll be there at 8:00." That means you'll make reasonable allowances for traffic and do everything in your power to show up on time. It does not guarantee that there won't be an earthquake that knocks out the freeway on which you're driving, or that you won't stop to help people injured in a traffic accident.

Commitment can be uncomfortable. Remember the high diving board? Can you recall the first time you stood up there and looked down? You may have had a moment of hesitation. And you may have felt stuck there for some period of time, mulling over a long list of unanswerable questions: Will the water be too cold? Too deep? Too shallow? Will I do a belly flop? If I do a belly flop, will anyone see it? What about rocks? Sharks? Life jackets? What am I doing here, anyway? And on and on, with anxiety possibly growing into full-blown paralysis. Weighing the pros and cons of jumping can keep you on the board forever.

Each time you are asked to commit, you may go through a similar process. Will I fail? Be exposed? Become overcommitted? What are the consequences of saying "No"? You may face fear of the unknown, resistance to change, feelings of being trapped, and the anxiety of giving up precious options. All these things come up when we consider commitment. We get in trouble and become paralyzed when we confuse our goal with the real or imagined obstacles to achieving that goal—and start thinking more about the obstacles than the goal.

When this hesitation at the end of the diving board is habitual, it becomes difficult to trust our own resolve. We may find ourselves asking, "Do I mean what I say, or not? How strong is my intention?" After a while, it becomes very difficult to trust other people as well. We begin to see their actions and intentions through our own lens of self-doubt, hesitancy, and mistrust.

So where does commitment occur? Commitment occurs when you are already off the end of the diving board—in a place where you no longer have a decision to make. It is a condition of no conditions. Instead of standing shivering on the high-dive, wasting energy by anxiously reviewing all the pros and cons of whether or not to jump, you have already determined that you *will* jump. Self-doubt, hesitancy, mistrust, and paralysis disappear because you no longer have to make the decision.

Commitment is a serious matter. It shouldn't be taken lightly. We should have every opportunity to consider what we are doing and to deal with our doubts before we make a commitment. Then, once the commitment is made, we can throw ourselves into it wholeheartedly.

## Honoring Doubt

Most problems with commitment happen at the time the commitment is *made*, not when it is being executed. We tend to make commitments too quickly, mostly because we're afraid—of offending someone by saying "No," of not going along with the program, of being seen as incompetent, or even of retribution. So some of the most important communications about commitment happen at the moment a commitment is being made.

Many random organizations actually encourage false commitments, especially when the only right answer is "Yes" to whatever is asked. When people don't have the freedom to doubt, and to weigh commitments before they make them, they wind up making commitments they know they can't keep. It may not be cool to say, "Can I have twenty-four hours and get back to you?" Instead, people do what the culture demands. They salute and say "Yes."

Then they're stuck at the top of the high-dive. They can't go back down the ladder, because the random organization insists that they commit to doing everything that is asked of them—but neither can they jump, because they're not really committed in their hearts. (Real commitments are always made in the heart. If people's hearts aren't in the commitment, it doesn't matter how many times they say "Yes.") So they can't jump, and they can't turn around and go back down the ladder. What are the options? They can stall for a while. They can go halfway, making excuses and collecting good reasons why they couldn't make good on the promise. They can say "Yes" and not give a time for completion. These are the ways commitments are usually handled in a random organization.

When there is pressure for high performance, and no room for doubt or consideration before making a commitment, one of the few options is to fake it. This is how pretended commitments spread through an organization. They are not malicious; they are the product of fear-based dynamics and teams that are not grounded in trust. And each pretended promise gets passed down through the organization until it gets to the customer.

In a trust-based organization, people have time to consider whether or not they can actually make a commitment, and it's safe to brainstorm alternatives. We need to learn to honor doubt in this new way. Doubt needs to come out of the closet and into the conference room, where it can be presented without prejudice. When doubt is denied, discouraged, or shut off, its effect is still felt—usually much later in the game when time, productivity, credibility, and trust have already been lost. When there is room for doubt and deliberation before decisions are made, then the commitments that people *do* make are more likely to be true commitments.

---

## FOLK THEOREM XV.

*Genuine doubt virtually always precedes real commitment.*

---

Ed, the art director for a large national nonprofit organization, was extremely busy with the annual summer ad campaign. In a casual hallway conversation, the director asked Ed if he could also manage a special fund-raiser during the same time period. In this particular nonprofit, the organizational culture dictated that Ed's response would be, "Sure! Of course!" That's exactly what he said, with the result that he and his staff experienced stress, burnout, frayed relationships, and a less than stellar artistic result with the ad campaign.

Later, when the organization began implementing the Trust Model and explored what was "cool" versus what was productive in the arena of hallway commitments, they decided to make room for recommending alternative solutions. In the new trust-based culture, Ed had permission to say, "Great idea! Can I get back to you within twenty-four hours with my answer?"

Leadership organizations respect the serious nature of commitments and provide generous opportunity to weigh carefully whether or not to make each commitment. They honor doubt as an invitation to examine the proposed commitment and to see if we can genuinely make the promise.

Some people ask, "But do I really need to think that much about making every commitment? What about agreeing to pick up milk on the way home?" For these folks, we make a distinction between a Type I error, which is looking for doubt that isn't really there, and a Type II error, which is *not* looking for doubt that really is there, lurking in the shadows. Type II errors are by far the more common problem in business. Type II errors are the big ones.

## Commitment Begins with Leadership

Returning to our diving board example, have you ever noticed what happens when one kid, usually bigger than the rest, just holds his nose and jumps? Everybody wants to be next. He opens a door. People see not only that he survived, but that he's something of a hero. The other kids start pushing to be the next one up the ladder and off the board.

When leadership models commitment, it becomes attractive. People see the results and productivity that come with it, and the admiration that people have for it. This encourages people to be the next off the diving board, despite their fears. At that point, more people in your organization become leaders.

When people trust that the commitments they make are genuine, and that the commitments others make are genuine, they start to believe in one another. Everybody becomes more efficient, because no energy is lost to wondering, worrying, and shivering at the end of the diving board. Trust spreads throughout the organization as people gain credibility with one another.

### *How to Support Authentic Commitments*

We suggest the following four ways to support people in making authentic commitments. You might look at them in light of your organization making a commitment to the Trust Model.

1. **Fashion a large, attractive vision that excites people.** Shape the commitment as a vision and place it in a larger context. Visions that excite people always have certain characteristics. First, they are a challenge. Second, they include not just a payback, but the reward of doing something that hasn't been done or hasn't been done as well before. And third, these visions have some measure of altruism in them. This first step is the motivation for getting people to jump off the diving board.

2. **Leadership jumps first.** Leadership takes the first risk, visibly, and then solicits participation from others. People often ask how leadership gets *itself* to jump. Imagine the person at the end of the diving board, struggling with all those questions. How do you go about deciding whether to jump or to go back down the ladder? First, you make a list of all your questions. You will discover that the answers fall into three categories: (*a*) you already know the answer; (*b*) you could get an answer with some research (asking someone, pilot project, etc.); or (*c*) you can't know the answer until you're in the water. That's the risk that everybody must share, and leadership has to do it first. When leadership models something, a critical mass of the organization usually follows.

3. **Get other team members to join in the risk.** This can be done through small groups in which people have a chance to ask leadership questions about the commitment. The leaders have probably asked and answered these same questions for themselves. This can be a very productive give-and-take, and input from these small groups may even alter the vision. If leadership runs into questions that they can't answer, they should just tell the truth, label this as the team's uncontrollable risk, and explain truthfully how leadership shares that risk.

4. **When you have buy-in, you have a strategic plan.** Once the first three steps are complete, the team will tell you exactly what strategic plan is needed to achieve the vision. This is a true top-down, bottom-up fusion of interests and activities, and the result is a true commitment.

These steps work more quickly and efficiently when trust is a core value in your organization, and this is something over which you have control.

## The Shift to Closure and Commitment

In the next chapter, we'll tell you *how* to make this shift. First, however, let's look at *why* it is not only possible but relatively simple to shift your organizational culture to one of closure and commitment using tactful, respectful communication.

Three powerful forces are working in your favor:

1. **Nonclosure and false commitments are habits, and habits can be changed.** We've seen that if one person changes his or her habit, the chance of closure increases. If two people change their habits, it increases even more. If the organization creates a conscious culture of closure, you have even more backup. Habits can be changed consciously through self-discovery, leadership modeling the standard, and creating an environment in which everyone stands for closure. Instead of training one another in nonclosure through self-perpetuating fear-based habits, we first recognize that nonclosure is only a habit, remind ourselves of the benefits of closure, work with the guidelines our organization adopts, and reinforce one another's new habits of closure and commitment.

Every benefit you receive from the Trust Model will be the result of a change in behavior. That is why the Trust Model constantly focuses on converting *unconscious habit* to *conscious behavior*. Usually, these behaviors result in moving every interaction toward closure, making only genuine commitments, and communicating in ways that promote closure and authentic commitment.

2. **Fear is less pervasive in a leadership organization, opening the door to closure and commitment.** Lack of closure is a fear-driven dynamic. It has nothing to do with the marketplace, with people being busy, or with anything other than fear-based habits. Fear plays a large part in what people are willing to communicate and what issues they are willing to close. What they communicate and close can be affected by fear of negative feedback, being wrong, being fired, being excluded or passed over, not being close to the boss, losing a friend, failure, embarrassment, not being accepted, looking stupid, and so on. All of these conditions are likely to decrease as you move toward being a leadership organization.

3. **You have the power to tip the balance between people's desire to contribute and their fear of doing so.** You can do this by modeling and fostering an atmosphere that favors closure, authentic commitment, and sound risk. One of these two emotions—the passion to contribute, or the fear of doing so—drives every interaction. By modeling closure and commitment, and implementing trust guidelines that support them, you can make it easier for people to pursue their desire to contribute than it is to give in to their fear, hesitation, and pessimism. You can invite people to the positive side of their natures, and most will go along if you also give them the skills to follow trust principles.

## Startup, Inc.

Closure and commitment were two of the first issues that surfaced at Startup, Inc. Randy, Startup's new CEO, had worked with trust-based teams, but he had never been exposed to the rapid movement and dramatic dynamics of a fiery new software startup. For the first three weeks of his tenure, he had a funny feeling that Damon, the founder who was in charge of sales, was avoiding him. Damon never quite seemed up to looking him in the eye, so Randy invited him out to dinner to find out what was going on.

Damon had very little experience with trust, and it took Randy until dessert to draw out the reason for Damon's anxiety. It seems that while Startup was courting investors, Damon sold his partner Trevor, the potential investors, and all the attorneys on the idea that he could produce $60 million in revenue the first year and $100 million a year in the second year. These were very unrealistic figures, and some of the investors asked for supporting material showing just how it could be done—but Damon always managed to put them off. Then, just as the first group of investors was backing away, another group began showing interest in Startup. The original investors were impressed with this group and didn't want to lose the deal. They made a grab for the company without ever seeing Damon's supporting materials, and Startup signed on the dotted line.

The lack of closure was that no one had ever demanded Damon's materials, and Damon had made a false commitment because he was afraid of not getting investors unless he inflated the figures.

Randy knew he had a mess on his hands, but he was relieved to have gotten to the bottom of the problem. He began by acknowledging Damon for having told him this uncomfortable truth. Next, he worked with Damon to come up with realistic figures and began taking the four steps to supporting authentic commitments that we described earlier.

Startup now had a vision that would excite people, because the revenue figures could actually be achieved. Randy modeled the commitment to them and asked Damon to see if he could truly commit to the new figures. He met with Damon and the sales force, and got their buy-in and a strategic plan for making those sales.

It was a good lesson for everyone, because they saw how much easier it would have been to start out with closure and commitment, rather than having to go back and pick up the pieces.

In the next chapter, we will look at the seven steps to closure in any interaction and see how they were implemented at Bigger, Inc.

# 6

# The Seven Steps
# to Closure

LEADERSHIP ORGANIZATIONS CREATE higher productivity, satisfaction, effectiveness, and profits by giving people both the motivation and the tools they need to close every interaction.

This chapter presents those tools—the seven steps to closure. The people in your organization can use these seven steps to train one another away from the widespread habit of nonclosure and move toward closure in every interaction so that they create "win-win" experiences consistently and begin to produce extraordinary results.

These seven steps are a system for getting closure even in organizations that have not practiced it before—whether that closure is between two individuals over a ham sandwich or encompasses a major organizational issue such as market direction. The steps include measures that people would naturally use to resolve issues, but also offer ways to understand how fear has been impeding closure, to identify ways in which each person has been participating in nonclosure, to focus attention on what each person can do to facilitate closure, and to define cycles properly.

In the early stages of working toward closure, we recommend following these steps explicitly. As you practice the process, you will find yourself following them automatically. As we describe each step, we will show how it was implemented at our composite organization, Bigger, Inc.

# Step 1: Clarify the Problem

The first step is to identify and clarify the problem. Naming the problem objectifies it, and objectifying something creates distance between us and it. This distance allows us to treat the unclosed issue consciously and systematically.

In this step, each individual involved thinks through a series of questions and writes down the answers:

1. **What is the unclosed issue, challenge, conflict, or misunderstanding?** The issue could range from "Where is my ham sandwich?" to "Will I get the raise?" or "Is the company being sold?" or "When will we have the sales figures?" or "Are Alice and I meeting next week?" or "Is the company going anywhere?" Any issue that makes you wonder or worry is unclosed. The more clearly you state the unclosed issue, the better start you have on closure.

2. **What are the reasons this issue hasn't been closed?** These might include "We're all too busy," "We're growing like crazy," "We have a personality conflict," or "We have other priorities." Also list what fears may be impacting your ability to reach closure with this situation. The simple act of naming our fears often reduces their influence. Fears might include "We don't want the boss to see us fighting," "You can't say that kind of thing in this company," or "The squeaky wheel doesn't get oiled, it gets fired." People often tell us they have fear about their ability, fear that their leadership will feel challenged, fear that an outcome won't be acceptable, fear that people will quit, fear that not having the right people in place makes them a bad leader, fear of financial outcome, fear of having to learn new things, fear of the unknown and of being out of control, fear that they can't solve a problem, and fear of embarrassment, humiliation, retribution, or conflict.

Fears can keep us from moving forward. Sometimes we leave a situation in limbo because we're afraid of a poor outcome. We can even try to deny that the problem exists, which only makes it persist and usually get worse. We need a certain amount of fear in order to survive—but we can't let habitual fear keep us from connecting with others and closing issues that need to be closed.

**3. What has this lack of closure cost in terms of productivity?** What is the cost in opportunity? Quality? What potential isn't being tapped? What crises are being generated unnecessarily? What customers are feeling frustrated? What is at risk?

What is the personal cost to you? Is it frustration? Burnout? Self-esteem? Worry? How does it affect your career? Does it spill over into other areas of your life? How is it affecting your customers, and how does that hurt you? Are you as effective as you might be? Are you giving as much as you could to the job? Are you treating customers as well as you might be treating them if you had closure on this issue? Are you thinking positively about your future in the organization?

The costs to the organization are usually obvious. People spend their time and energy on "Them vs. Us" and muck, rather than on making, supporting, and selling the product or service, development, recruiting, marketing, or other productive channels.

The personal cost is sometimes less obvious. When people don't have closure, they are less likely to invest their energy, talents, will, and enthusiasm at work. They go through the motions and do enough to keep their jobs, but they don't go the extra mile, don't contribute beyond what is required, and bring only what is absolutely necessary to work. This makes for low satisfaction and low productivity, which can affect careers as well as self-esteem.

**4. How have you been participating in the roadblock of nonclosure—through action, nonaction, or both?** What are you doing, or not doing, that is part of the problem? This can be an uncomfortable area to explore, but it is also the way out of the problem. For example, we sometimes participate by being "too busy," by procrastinating, or by not using direct communication. And if open or accurate communication isn't being used, then what *is* being used? Almost always, the answer is buzzing. We need some form of expression, and we look for it in indirect ways if direct communication is not in play. In that way, we contribute to the problem.

Sometimes we participate in the problem by *not* acting or speaking. We stand apart, arms folded, looking critically at the situation and shaking our heads. We may or may not be buzzing about it with others, but we are doing nothing to fix it. "It's not my job to do that. . . . They made the mess; let them fix it. . . . It's none of my business. . . ." In a leadership organization, anyone who *sees* lack of closure is invested in urging the issue toward closure—and people support one another in doing this.

In a random organization, people often participate in the problem by trying to avoid it in some way. They simply don't want to face the issue because it's too difficult, unpleasant, hopeless, or uncomfortable. True leaders make it their business to understand what makes these people uncomfortable and why, so that their discomfort doesn't keep them from acting when it's appropriate for them to act. They learn to keep their attention on the outcome, rather than on the obstacles to the outcome.

Another way people become part of the problem is by not delegating and trying to keep all the applause for themselves. Or they may not follow up when they know they need to do so. Or they might go around their boss, communicating not to him or her, but to someone else.

5. **What could you do instead to move things toward closure?** You may need to start a conversation about the issue that isn't closed—the project, the direction of the company, the merger, or whatever it is that makes you wonder or worry. You may need to give answers to someone who is wondering or worrying about an issue over which *you* have control. You may need to take an uncomfortable action that you've been avoiding—hiring a new advertising agency or marketing consultant, replacing key people, or having a difficult conversation with your boss or with someone who works for you. You may need to make tough decisions even before you have those conversations.

By when will you do it? Part of closure is having a date for completion, or at least a date for initiation. That is the final piece of information that gives everyone certainty about what is going to happen.

As you answer these questions, the problem usually becomes very clear. If you are having trouble getting clear even at this point, something may be standing in the way—for you or for others involved in this process with you. Some of the most common obstacles to closure are:

• **Procrastination.** Procrastination is never a result of being too busy. It is almost always an attempt to avoid the issue or to put off something that appears to be uncomfortable, painful, or hopeless. When someone tells you that he or she is "too busy," dig a little deeper to see the pain or difficulty that is being avoided. Underneath your pain, you may see a habit. It is critical to remember that habits lurk beneath our avoidance behavior.

• **Being rigid and demanding.** We sometimes project an image or style that unintentionally or unconsciously invites others to choose fear over the vision—so that their fear keeps them from reaching closure.

• **Avoiding conflict.** Conflict is uncomfortable, so uncomfortable that some people endure the pain of staying in the problem rather than confront their fear of conflict.

## The Closure Problem at Bigger, Inc.

The problem of nonclosure had been growing at Bigger, Inc., for some time. A few years earlier, they'd had a corner on the market and were doing very well. They had a typical hierarchical organizational structure in which information and orders flowed from the top downward and input from individual employees was not perceived as welcome. The company had developed an attitude of entitlement, as if they deserved the top market share. The lack of competition had made them lazy, and these habits of laziness and entitlement became part of their interactions with one another as well.

Nonclosure and pretended commitments sprawled out across the organization, with the inevitable rise of "Them vs. Us" dynamics. The situation came to a head in the problem described in Chapter 3 between Pat, the CFO, and Alex, the vice president of sales, over forecasting the sales figures. The two "Them vs. Us" cliques that emerged from this difficulty poked at one another for months. Alex, Ted (human resources), and Max (business planning) lined up against Pat,

Sam (the CEO), Jan (sales administration), Sheryl (marketing), and Randy (operations) on several issues.

On the surface, it appeared that the latter clique had more power—but as they discovered, a team without all its members isn't a very productive team. Just a few dissenters, and only a little "Them vs. Us" as a result of nonclosure, can bring a company to a standstill. No one at Bigger, Inc., could get accurate information, no one knew what was really going on, and so no one could plan effectively. And this was only the outer problem. On the inner, emotional plane, morale plummeted because it was almost impossible to do a good job under these circumstances.

When sales forecasting went out of whack, the whole company was thrown off balance. Product distribution, operations, sales, sales administration, finance, marketing, and business development were only a few of the divisions affected. Confusion and lack of closure bred more "Them vs. Us" throughout the company. The cliques expanded and splintered. Some days, it seemed that nobody was on the same team.

When we began working with Bigger, Inc., we developed this partial list of functions and groups among whom some degree of "Them vs. Us" had occurred. It included almost all the possibilities listed in Chapter 3:

- finance and sales
- sales and engineering
- business development and marketing
- operations and packaging
- business development and operations
- engineering and operations
- quality and operations
- sales and marketing
- sales and sales administration
- quality and engineering
- distribution and packaging
- conflicts within senior management

Max, the head of business planning, had tried to solve the problem with an OEM (Original Equipment Manufacturer) deal whereby another company would integrate and distribute a certain amount of Bigger's product. Everybody in the industry was trying to capture these OEM deals, because they made life so much easier. All the company had to do was make the product. For a price, the OEM company would take it off your hands and do all the selling and distributing.

Max lined up two major, multimillion-dollar OEM deals. But because Bigger was riddled with "Them vs. Us" dynamics, nonclosure, pretended commitments, and flawed communication, they failed to keep their commitments on the OEM deals and lost *both* of them. They failed with the OEMs because they were failing with one another within the company. They weren't closing their interactions or keeping their commitments with one another, so they didn't close their interactions or keep their commitments with the OEMs. So, having finally secured these deals, Bigger blew them both.

### Step 1 at Bigger, Inc.

This was the situation when we began working with Bigger. They had started calling their situation "the communication problem." It was a blanket phrase they used for the condition of splintered cliques, lack of trust, and decreased market share. The smaller problem of Pat and Alex's disagreement had long since been enveloped in the mushrooming inability of some individuals or departments at Bigger to communicate honestly with one another.

They were committed to finding solutions, and we started taking them through the seven steps to closure. We began with Step 1: Clarify the Problem. The crisis had occurred when they lost the OEM deals, but it was important for them to see that the real problem underlying all their difficulties was the lack of closure and the resulting "Them vs. Us" dynamics and pretended commitments.

First, everyone on the lead team—Sam, Pat, Alex, Ted, Max, Randy, Jan, and Sheryl—answered the five questions mentioned earlier for identifying and clarifying the problem. It was uncomfortable, but each person looked at what issues hadn't been closed, the reasons they hadn't been closed, their fears about closing them, what it was costing both Bigger and themselves as individuals not to have closure, how they had been participating in the nonclosure, and what they were willing to do about it.

When they came together in their Step 1 lead-team meeting, they quickly realized that improving communication at Bigger was an enormous task and that they would have to break it down into smaller, more understandable components. They even went so far as to create a grid that defined the problem according to strategic and tactical components and functional and nonfunctional components. Strategic components, of course, meant the overall, long-term aspects of the situation. Tactical components were short-term methods for achieving their goals. Functional elements meant that the situation related to a specific department, and nonfunctional meant that it did not.

## Problem Defining Grid

|  | Nonfunctional | Functional |
|---|---|---|
| Strategic | Company Vision | New Products |
|  | Company Goals | New Technologies |
|  | Company Culture | Priorities |
|  |  | Resources |
|  |  | Schedules |
| Tactical | Customer Priorities | Status of Issues |
|  | Revenue Goals | Customers |
|  | Competition Offerings | Development |
|  | Company Changes | Testing |
|  |  | Schedules |
|  |  | Reporting |

This grid allowed the lead team to perceive their problem more clearly. Only when they could see the road ahead could they start moving. Prior to making this grid, "the communication problem" had seemed like an unapproachable miasma of muck. By breaking it down into its components, they could look at it more realistically and start tackling one thing at a time.

The issues you need to close may not be as large or complex as "the communication problem" at Bigger. It may be as simple as "Do we, or do we not, open a particular market?" In this case, you and the others involved will simply write down your answers to the five questions in Step 1 and go on to Step 2.

# Step 2: Create the Vision

Your vision is a specific picture of what you want to happen. It tells how you want the "movie" to end and gives you a goal that you will recognize when you get there.

## *Be Specific*

Create a specific picture of what success would look like in your organization. The more specific you make your vision, the more likely you are to be successful—even if you change the details of your vision partway through the movie. Your vision could include your own wants and needs and also the wants and needs of your customers and stakeholders.

Research shows that we get dramatic improvement in performance when we first create clear visions. These studies have dealt largely with sports and healing, but the same principles apply in business. There is a big difference between envisioning revenue of $500 million and a market capitalization of $2 billion—and the vision you choose will affect the choices you make and the actions you take.

Be specific about the result you want, not just the means to getting it. One Olympic athlete spent months envisioning herself walking out on the tarmac representing her country in the opening ceremonies parade. That vision became reality, but what she had *not* envisioned was herself standing on the winners' podium receiving a medal—and that *didn't* happen. She returned four years later with a different vision and accomplished her real dream of winning a medal.

In the same way, envisioning "better communications" within your team at work may lead to disappointment if what you really want is the *result* of better communications—greater productivity, satisfaction, and profits. Your team may sit around communicating beautifully all day, but if it stops there, you won't get the result you want.

As you shape your vision, move from the broad to the narrow. You might move, for instance, from "better communications" to:

- We want better communication in the following areas:
  _____.
- Better communication in these areas would lead to closure on these specific issues: _____.
- We will know we have closure in these areas because we will see: _____.

The more specific you make your vision, the more likely you are to reach closure. "I want to reach closure with Charlie Jones on who is handling the Lambert deal" produces a better result than "Fix things with Charlie."

## Be Courageous

Some of us have trouble being explicit because we're afraid of how our ideas will be received. We don't want to be rejected, and we think that people are less likely to react negatively to our vision if we blur it a little around the edges or present it in such general language that no one could possibly have a problem with it.

"We propose creating an environment in which everybody gets more satisfaction and is more productive" is a very general vision. Nobody could argue with it, but how are these results going to be produced? How would you know if you had achieved it? And if nothing specific is done, will any specific results be produced?

"We propose a culture in which interactions are closed 100 percent of the time" might generate some fearful reactions at first, but once people have had a chance to work through the defenses common to all of us and thus actually embrace the proposal, they will get specific results.

### Step 2 at Bigger, Inc.

When you have clarified the problem, it is easier to create the vision. The lead team at Bigger sat down and came up with a five-point vision:

- Develop processes required to ensure accurate, timely, and appropriate generation, collection, dissemination, storage, and disposition of company information and information about specific programs.
- Establish critical links among people, functions, ideas, and information that are necessary for success.
- Learn good communication so that everyone involved is prepared to send and receive communications in a "common language" and understands how their individual communications affect the company's culture.
- Close 100 percent of all interactions and communications throughout the company.
- Make no false or pretended promises.

## Step 3: Communication

In order to reach closure, you need to talk to the other people involved with the issue. These conversations should be aimed at resolving whatever muck has accumulated between you and at coming to clear commitments about who will do what, and by when.

One of the most common reasons for nonclosure is that people put off having conversations they're afraid will be uncomfortable. Sometimes these closure conversations *are* uncomfortable, but not having them only makes the situation worse. The issue never gets closed, and the relationship they were trying to protect inevitably deteriorates in the wake of nonclosure. It's easier in the long run just to bite the bullet and have the conversation.

Steps 1 and 2 prepare you to communicate. You have clarified the problem and created the vision, so you're in a much better position to communicate. Step 3 consists of a series of one-on-one meetings or meetings among several people. These meetings take place between people who have become involved in "Them vs. Us" dynamics, people whose functions appear to be in conflict, and/or people who need to work together on solutions.

The dyads or groups meet to clear the air, to discuss the issues that were clarified in Step 1, and to find solutions that are in alignment with the vision created in Step 2. Each group is asked to write down the options they considered and their recommendations for a solution. Then everybody comes together in a leadership executive meeting to decide which options and recommendations are best for the organization.

Obviously, all of these contacts will go more smoothly and be more productive when people are using the closure communications skills described in Chapter 5.

To be consistently successful and effective with closure communication, people need specific, formal communication training. They also need to see that good closure communication requires both mechanics and intention. *Mechanics* are the technical aspects of communication: knowing the difference between an assumptive question and a nonassumptive question, not interrupting, and so on. Mechanics are important, but it's even more important to approach communication with the *intention* for everybody to win and to reach closure. When that intention is in place, you will naturally apply mechanics that work.

Only when closure communications have taken place, both in small dyads and in the larger group meeting, can you go on to Step 4, Reach Consensus.

### Step 3 at Bigger, Inc.

For Step 3, the lead team at Bigger made an extensive list of people who needed to talk to one another with a facilitator present and set up a series of one-on-one meetings. Pat and Alex, for instance, obviously needed to talk. Jan, of sales administration, also needed to sit down with Alex and Pat. And Ted in human resources needed to sit down with "bean-counting" Randy of operations. As CEO, Sam needed to meet with several people.

Sheryl of marketing also needed to sit down with many people in the aftermath of her role as "go-between" courting favor with both of the two original cliques. Ted needed to talk with Pat about problems they'd had in the past. Max of business planning needed to talk to almost everybody about throwing a monkey wrench into his carefully crafted OEM deal—but he especially needed to talk with Sam, who had gone around him on some important aspects of the deals.

These were some of the pairings for small meetings:

- Pat and Alex (CFO and sales)
- Alex and Jan (sales and sales administration)
- Alex and Sam (sales and CEO)
- Ted and Randy (human resources and operations)
- Randy and Alex (operations and sales)
- Sam and Ted (CEO and human resources)
- Pat and Ted (CFO and human resources)
- Sheryl and Alex (marketing and sales)
- Sheryl and Sam (marketing and CEO)
- Sam and Pat (CEO and CFO)
- Pat and Jan (CFO and sales administration)
- Sheryl and Pat (marketing and CFO)
- Max and Sam (business planning and CEO)
- Max and Alex (business planning and sales)
- Max and Pat (business planning and CFO)

Each of these dyads was given an issue from the grid that needed to be closed, and everyone was asked to write down their options and recommendations. Some of these meetings were very dicey, and it helped to have a facilitator present. Everyone found that practicing the communication skills we've described not only helped them resolve the muck and reach closure, but made them feel more at peace with the process and excited about the prospect of better communication in the future.

When they all came together in the large group, everyone was amazed at the number and quality of proposals people had brought with them. The next step was to reach consensus.

# Step 4: Reach Consensus

Successful communication brings you to consensus on how to close the issue or issues you are considering. Consensus means that a critical mass of the people involved are committed to the action that has been proposed—whether or not they completely agree with it.

In a one-on-one discussion, consensus usually means agreement. In a group of more than two people, consensus only requires that

1. Everyone's views have been heard and considered

2. The outcome is explained by the final decision-makers

3. People can align behind the decision, regardless of whether or not they are in full agreement with it

Consensus is neither unanimity nor majority rule. Again, it means agreeing *to*, not necessarily agreeing *with*, the solution that has been proposed. Most people will consent to a good idea that is not their own if their own ideas have been heard and openly considered. On most teams, unanimity isn't possible. Requiring that decisions be unanimous only invites false commitment.

The large meeting when everybody comes together to reach consensus about how to close an issue is a connected team's payoff time. Everybody gets to voice his or her opinion. Sometimes the discussion becomes overheated, and you may need to take a break. If the disagreements slip out of productive channels, simply identify any additional information you may need and set a date and time to reconvene. Ideally, the team holds the tension among all the different points of view well enough, and long enough, that a new synthesis emerges. The team's highest intelligence has then been discovered, and everybody can get together behind the group's best ideas.

There is a moment in these meetings, or in any individual closure communication, when the air clears. Everybody recognizes this moment, consciously or unconsciously. Emotions and tensions have been released, views have been shared, collaboration is working, and suddenly clarity emerges about what to do. A critical mass of the people present see a way to close the issue so that everybody wins.

The emotional experience of this moment is the opposite of muck's emotional impact. It is elevating, energizing, and releasing. You know you have found something that would have been available through no other path. Yet this moment is neither magical nor accidental, fleeting nor subtle. It is clearly recognizable if you are looking for it, and you can re-create the experience time after time using trust principles and trust communication. When this moment of clarity occurs—again, when people experience the possibility of a win-win outcome—it's time to acknowledge the consensus so that you can move forward to devising strategies.

The facilitator should check with everybody to make sure they have felt the moment of consensus. Often, this is simply a matter of going around the room and saying, "Can you live with this? Can you commit to this, even though it's different from your suggestion?"

Each team needs to arrive at its own definition of consensus. Who needs to agree, and to what type of decision? Does anybody have a veto? Do you need the board's consent as well? Some organizations use "consensus with a CEO veto" because the CEO is usually more accountable to the board and stockholders than anybody else—but when this option is in place, there are usually requirements that the CEO explain the veto in writing and in some detail.

## Step 4 at Bigger, Inc.

The lead team at Bigger sat around the table for a long time discussing the written proposals that each dyad had brought with them to the meeting. At times, tension filled the air. At other times, a ripple of laughter broke unexpectedly through the group. People looked around sheepishly, unaccustomed to sharing humor or agreement on the tough issues.

Various groups and dyads had been assigned to make recommendations on each of the elements in the grid they constructed in Step 1: company vision, goals, and culture; new products and technologies; priorities; resources; schedules; customer priorities; revenue goals; competition offerings; company changes; and status of issues, customers, development, testing, schedules, and reporting. It took quite a while to cover all these areas, but as the team worked together using closure communication skills, they began to come together in their thinking. There were disagreements, but everyone began to get a sense that they were a team working together toward a common goal—the vision they had worked out in Step 2. They had worked through many of their individual differences and battles between functions in Step 3, and that had helped clear the way for consensus as well.

At one point in the discussion, the moment of consensus seemed to settle over the team. It was clear that people still held different points of view, but it was also clear that they were all seeing things from the perspective of what was best for the company. What was best for the company was usually clear, regardless of the variations on that theme presented by individual people and functions. A feeling of alignment began to emerge, an overall approach to their situation that was going to work for everyone. When that approach became apparent and its components started to become clear, the facilitator went around the table and asked everyone, "Can you live with this?"

The answer was "Yes," and then everyone looked around at one another in silence. They were a little stunned that they had actually reached consensus, but it was obvious to everyone around the table that they had.

# Step 5: Devise Strategies

Your strategies are your action plan. After consensus is reached in Step 4, devising strategies is simply a matter of coming up with the actions that will produce the results on which the team has already agreed.

One of the key differences between random organizations and leadership organizations is that random organizations try to devise strategies before completing Steps 1 through 4. They bypass the potential discomfort or conflict involved in these steps, and in doing so, they subvert the process. They never define what the problem really is, let alone create a vision, communicate for closure, or reach consensus. The result is they devise strategies without first resolving the fundamental issues that caused the problem in the first place. It's no wonder these solutions rarely work, or work only for a short time.

Even when they do reach closure, the result is likely to be win-lose. The classic example of this process is the old labor/management wars. When companies went straight into contract "negotiations" without first establishing a win-win attitude through Steps 1–4, the contract might get signed—but both sides immediately started storing up ammunition for the next battle.

As with everything that happens in a culture of trust, coming up with strategies that stay workable is more than an intellectual exercise. People need to buy in at an emotional, as well as a conceptual, level.

## Step 5 at Bigger, Inc.

Since Bigger had such a wide range of issues, let's look at just one. The first issue on the grid was that company vision, goals, and culture were not clear. The strategies on which the group reached consensus were:

- establish and promote a company Trust Model statement
- quarterly objectives "cascaded" from corporate level to VPs, directors, managers, supervisors, and individual contributors
- monthly meetings with the executive board, with conclusions and assignments rendered in writing
- mandate regular staff communications between VPs, directors, managers, and their staffs
- mandate regular one-on-ones, with written closure statements
- initiate one-on-ones that skip levels in the organizational chart
- make communications with management, peers, and subordinates a measure for performance reviews

These were the action items, or strategies, for the first quadrant on the grid.

# Step 6: Distribute Accountabilities

This step creates the actual closure, because it says who will do what, and by when. Having developed your strategies in Step 5, you now assign the tasks. Step 6 is a written statement of who is accountable, by when the action will be taken, the resources necessary to complete the action, and strategies for getting whatever buy-in will be necessary.

Some people have an odd resistance to putting things in writing. It's as if they're thinking, "Don't you trust me?" Actually, putting closure plans into writing is a gesture of trust. It says that we all believe in what we agreed to do and value the outcome enough to make it official. Closure statements also help avoid the muck of discovering later that there was not, in fact, full agreement and that people remember the outcome differently from one another. Writing things down is teamwork savvy. It respects the fact that muck is always a possibility and doesn't rush into arrangements that invite it.

After all the various tasks have been assigned and completion dates determined, people fill out forms like the one on page 125 for each action item. Next, they give the forms to the person we call "the Horse." The Horse is the person who has ultimate responsibility for coordinating everybody's actions, although he or she is not necessarily the senior person on the team. The Horse has a master form that shows the exact status of each item at all times. He or she is responsible for following up to make sure deadlines are being met.

This form is your blueprint for success. Occasionally, we also ask people to identify what the benefits of success would be and to describe some of their fears about failure.

It's a simple fact that commitments with accountability tend to succeed, while those without accountability usually fail. Being accountable for the commitments we make is a skill that everyone in a leadership organization has to have, and it's a skill that usually requires training, practice, and an atmosphere that supports us in being accountable.

In a leadership organization, senior management leads the way to accountability in several ways:

- It creates the vision.
- It models being willing to make true commitments.

- It is explicitly accountable to the rest of the organization for its commitments.
- It provides the gift of performance pressure, balanced with support and acknowledgment.
- It initiates specific guidelines for the culture of closure.
- It provides the training required for a critical mass of the workforce to understand what effective commitments are and how to keep them.
- When any of these elements are missing in any significant way, the result is a random organization.

## Step 6 Accountability Closure Form

Vision _____

Today's Date _____

Date for Achievement _____

Probable Financial Impact (savings, revenues)_____

Buy-In Strategy (who, what, how, when)_____

Resources/Support Needed _____

Ultimate Accountability (The Horse)_____

| Action | By Whom | By When |
|--------|---------|---------|
| _____ | _____ | _____ |
| _____ | _____ | _____ |
| _____ | _____ | _____ |
| _____ | _____ | _____ |
| _____ | _____ | _____ |
| _____ | _____ | _____ |
| _____ | _____ | _____ |

### Step 6 at Bigger, Inc.

Each task that the Bigger team agreed to do was logged into a form like the one above. Pat became the Horse, because of her competence with detail.

One of the strategy items, "Establish and promote a company Trust Model statement," was assigned to Sam. He made a list of everything he would have to do, all the people with whom he would have to consult, and established a timeline for finishing the project. He filled out a form like the one on page 125 and gave a copy to Pat, who entered the information on her master form.

Everyone who received an accountability assignment did the same, and everyone had access to the master form so that they could see the big picture.

## Step 7: Handling Slippage

What do you do when slippage occurs? There are two kinds of slippage: the kind that results from a soft commitment, and the kind that results from a firm commitment that ran into reality. Both must be addressed immediately. The most expensive error people make is noticing slippage but hoping it will improve and not saying anything about it. This only contributes to the atmosphere of denial and nonclosure. The longer we put off tackling an awkward or difficult situation, the harder it is to address.

What are the consequences of not keeping your commitment that was soft to begin with? First, you have lost time. You have to go back and remake the commitment, or decide how to remedy the situation. And you have to take everybody on the team back with you to revisit the issue. Second, you lose trust. People have seen that you didn't keep the commitment once, and so you may have shorter times between check-ins, with the result that you may feel micromanaged. The biggest consequence, however, is loss of credibility—not only with your coworkers, subordinates, and managers, but with your customers. Remember, your credibility with your customer is only as strong as your credibility with the other people in your organization.

Nevertheless, slippage is a fact of life on any ambitious team, so it is useful to have an established method for dealing with it.

In a leadership organization, everyone is responsible for catching his or her own slippage. When people are about to slip, they are obligated to notify everybody who will be affected—immediately. We almost always know when we are going to slip. One clue is that we hear the excuses gathering in our minds. When that happens, we need to let people know. They may be able to help, and at the very least they have some warning. When people know they are about to slip and say nothing, they are involved in a pretended commitment from that moment on.

One way to help people catch slippage early is to have everyone bring the status of their action items, in writing, to every meeting. This takes accountability out of the "parent-child" realm. Everyone is an adult, and nobody has to "ride herd" on anyone else. It allows the team to forecast slippage with one another, rather than forcing them to be punitive with one another. Forecasting is important, because slippage can often be avoided with some warning.

The best way to handle slippage is right away, with respect, and in a way that builds trust. You don't want to tear people down, but to help them get back on track. Again, you want to create a win-win situation for everyone involved. Before you begin to address the slippage, remember how sensitive we all are to embarrassment or humiliation. Most of these conversations can take place in private, either with the Horse or with the people most directly involved with the action item.

Remember, the nonassumptive question "What happened?" is a far more effective method than the assumptive "What went wrong?" or even "Why did this happen?" Both of these latter questions invite defensiveness, and defensiveness delays moving forward. "What happened?" on the other hand, begins a respectful problem-solving collaboration. Not only that, but knowing what happened—the real status of the situation or circumstances surrounding the issue—can help you make intelligent choices about what to do.

Whenever there is slippage, you have four choices:

1. End the commitment, or end this person's involvement with it.

2. Change the commitment (change the timeline, resource allocation, etc.).

3. Recommit to the original accountability and timeline.

4. Ignore the situation and hope it will go away.

The last option spells disaster—but it is an option frequently selected, consciously or unconsciously. Choice 4 amounts to hoping the problem will go away on its own, hoping someone or something will change and *then* we'll make a real choice, imagining that we have been victimized or manipulated into an undesirable position, or letting outside circumstances ("the market," for instance) decide for us.

When we make choice 4, the problem persists. The only difference is that it gets harder and harder to approach. The marginal performance that caused the slippage is reinforced, and the entire process reverts to being a pretended or false commitment. It becomes clear that the team does not intend to do what it said it would do.

The other three choices all mean reexamining the commitment to one extent or another. When you get the answer to "What happened?" be sure to assess the facts and the performance, not the person. Make sure that you look for a choice that reestablishes a win-win outcome, not one that punishes the person. Your job is not to judge, but simply to understand the other person's point of view. You may need to reassess the person's willingness, ability, or level of aspiration, and to consider trial periods for second chances, but approach the first failure with a positive attitude. Assume that the person can and will do better. Find out how to help (without taking the problem back) and agree to supply what you can. Then reach closure by opting for choice 1, 2, or 3.

Ideally, the person accountable for the slipping item should bring to your meeting a written description of what happened and written recommendations about what to do. Choice 1 may be appropriate if the action turns out to be either impossible or irrelevant. Choice 2 may be a matter of applying more resources or establishing a new timeline. Or the item may be somewhat different from what you thought it was and may need someone else's expertise. In this case, you can transfer the accountability to another person. Choice 3 may be right if unusual circumstances that surrounded the issue are no longer in play.

When you have made your choice, put it in writing. Again, this isn't a gesture of mistrust, but an affirmation of the new agreement with guidelines of what support will be added—when, and by whom. The accountable person may need to check in with someone else on the team more often to report on progress.

What happens when someone consistently breaks promises, does not honor commitments, and is not accountable? You will need to begin a new conversation with this person. Start by pointing out that his or her words are not being matched by actions. Establish a trial period in which the person is given a very clear way to win and a very clear way to lose. Make sure the team supplies all the support it can. This makes it *supported* accountability, not *demanded* accountability. If the person still fails, it may be time to end that person's participation on the team, or at least consider choice 1 for this particular project.

The keys to handling slippage in a way that builds trust are respect, self-forecasting, addressing the issue immediately, making good choices based on facts, and getting the key elements in writing.

### Step 7 at Bigger, Inc.

Bigger was fortunate in that one of the first items to slip was being handled by Sam, the CEO. The way he dealt with the issue modeled handling slippage for the entire team and made it easier for them to manage the uncomfortable parts of this important step when their turn came to deal with slippage.

Sam was accountable for the action item "Establish and promote a company Trust Model statement." He had made a list of the people with whom he wanted to consult on the board, the lead team, and in middle management even before he began the five phases of implementing a Trust Model that we describe later in this book, but he was having two problems. First, the timeline was slipping because Sam was traveling extensively. Second, people seemed reluctant to speak frankly when he did sit down with them. Several board members seemed to be working their own agendas with him, and he suspected that both the lead team and middle management were telling him only what they thought he wanted to hear. The result was that he didn't feel he was getting good, truthful interviews, and he could see that he was not going to complete his work by the date he had promised.

Sam did exactly the right thing. As soon as he realized what was happening, he wrote it up and brought it to the next lead-team meeting with a recommendation that someone else head up this particular task. He felt that his position as CEO prevented him from getting the best, most honest responses in the interviews, and also that his current travel schedule was causing the timeline to slip. He recommended that Sheryl, of marketing, take over for him. She had good people skills, and her position wouldn't be as intimidating as his had been. The team decided that this was a good solution, gave Sheryl an adjusted timeline, and they were off and running again.

Another option would have been choice 2, changing the commitment. The interviews that Sam proposed were not strictly necessary. Bigger could have gone directly to the five phases of implementation described in Part IV of this book and created a more direct path to their Trust Model statement.

The seven steps we've discussed in this chapter guide you to a closure that works. As you and the people in your organization practice them, they start to become second nature. They become part of how you think and how you relate to one another.

Closure is the very foundation of a leadership organization. When a critical mass of people in your organization understand the value of closure, are given the skills to practice it consistently, and hold one another accountable for it, then you have a culture that gives you an unbeatable competitive advantage.

We've seen that fear is often at the bottom of nonclosure. The next chapter is about minimizing fear in your organization and dealing with it effectively when it arises.

# 7

# Antidotes to Fear

FEAR LIES JUST beneath the surface of much of the nonclosure we find in organizations. Anything we can do to minimize fear, anything that acts as an antidote to the fears we all experience, works in favor of closure, trust, and becoming a leadership organization.

We can't eliminate fear, and we wouldn't want to do so even if we could. Fear is part of our nature and our survival mechanism—but there is a difference between having fears and acting on them habitually, automatically, and unconsciously. We can keep fear from stopping us simply by becoming aware of how it operates and following specific trust principles.

Again, we need to understand fear before we can face it directly and harvest the benefits through closure, commitment, and communication.

## The Nature of Fear

Fear assaults us from two directions. First, there is our natural inborn fear, a survival mechanism to warn us of danger. Second, we all have experiences in our personal pasts that influence our behavior and make us fearful today. Some of these are the "never again" experiences described in Chapter 4. Behaviors that come out of "never again" experiences are usually habitual and automatic, like withdrawing our hand from fire, taking place without much input from our conscious minds.

So fear grips us in its pincers: one side rising out of our negative personal imprinting and the other side from our collective history as a species. Fear has an earlier and deeper presence than some of the positive emotions, giving it an unfair advantage over such aspirations as trust, meaning, and connection.

We don't want to feel fear, and so we often deny that it exists. The denial, of course, feeds it more power. It's difficult to talk about fear, and we're trained not to do so. Most team members say that fear is not an issue, but we have never encountered a single team on which fear did not have some adverse effect. Fear is like an iceberg. Its bulk is below the surface—and it isn't that nice bright, shiny stuff on top that punches a hole in the hull of the organization, it's what's below the water.

## Fear and Closure

We know that we stand poised between our passion to contribute and our fear of what will happen if we move in that direction—and that what tips the balance is trust. If this is true, then trying to increase productivity using fear is an astonishing tactic. It's like trying to raise one end of a seesaw by sitting on it. We prefer to push down on the other end, to reduce the effect of fear by neutralizing it with its opposite, trust. That takes courage, the courage to become aware of how fear operates in us and in our team and the courage to choose another path consciously and deliberately.

We all have fear-driven attitudes and actions, and these attitudes and actions are locked in habitual patterns like a virus lying hidden in the body, awaiting its next opportunity. At the individual level, these fear patterns are usually the blind spots associated with our "never again" decisions. At the team level, they are often lodged in "Them vs. Us" attitudes and limiting beliefs.

Here is our dilemma. It's not possible, reasonable, or even appropriate to wait until we've eliminated all our individual and team fear patterns before aspiring to improve team performance. That approach would take too long and, in the case of individual fears, require intervention that would be intrusive.

Instead, we can eliminate a huge percentage of our unconscious fear-driven patterns simply by *increasing closure* across the organization. Closure eliminates wondering, the breeding ground for suspicion and fear. Paradoxically, fear often keeps us from reaching closure. We may be afraid that if we press people to say who will do what, and by when, we risk being rejected, passed over, shouted down, criticized, fired, or humiliated. So there is a closed-loop relationship between increased closure and diminished fear. The more you increase closure, the more you diminish fear. The more you diminish fear, the more you increase closure.

By concentrating on closing every communication, and thereby raising the level of trust in the team, we bring unconscious, fear-based habits to light. When we do that, they lose their power to govern our behavior.

Minimizing fear is a bottom-up, top-down, and across-the-organization process. Bottom-up means that each individual develops the skills to avoid participating in nonclosure. Top-down means that the organization does not punish sound risk that fails, that it communicates openly and honestly with employees, deals with change in a clear and straightforward way, and consciously acts and speaks in ways that reduce fear, rather than increase it. Across-the-organization minimizing of fear means that everyone focuses on eradicating "Them vs. Us" dynamics and escaping the bondage of limiting beliefs.

Each of these three "directional" ways of minimizing fear reinforces the others. People find it easier to shoulder their personal responsibility when the organization is clearing away its own roadblocks. When all of this takes place within the context of the Trust Model, you have a secure framework for the team's interior life.

We find that one of the best ways to deal with fear is on the cognitive level. When we examine our fears rationally, it's obvious that many of them are irrational (e.g., once burned by a hot stove, we often avoid the whole kitchen). This is often how we deal with fear in our children. We simply explain that there isn't a monster in the closet, and we turn on the light to reveal the empty closet. The "just do it" strategy is also effective. In *Feel the Fear and Do It Anyway*, Susan Jeffers says that "pushing through fear is less frightening than living with the underlying fear that comes from a feeling of helplessness."[1]

---

1 Susan Jeffers, *Feel the Fear and Do It Anyway* (New York: Fawcett Books, 1992).

Understanding how fear works, the forms it takes, and what we are likely to do in the face of these fears are the first steps in changing our habits. Let's look first at individual fear.

## Individual Fear

As individuals, we experience a wide variety of fears. Following are some fears that people have reported to us:

- of retribution
- of rejection
- of the unknown
- of conflict
- of getting more work
- of looking stupid/weak/foolish/uncreative/uncool
- of not knowing the "answer"
- of not being acknowledged
- of responsibility
- of being too visible
- of being invisible
- of failure or, worse, getting caught failing
- of criticism
- of embarrassment
- of loss of friendship
- of being wrong
- of losing
- of winning (they'll just raise the bar)
- of hurting someone else's feelings
- of truth
- of being accountable
- of being isolated
- of not getting what I want
- of getting what I want (and then having to perform)

Jeffers speaks of Level 1 fears, which have to do with events or actions (accidents, public speaking), and Level 2 fears, which are associated with ego (rejection, loss of image). She goes on to say that the Level 3 fear, the fear underlying all other fears and the granddaddy fear of them all, is "I can't handle it!" This is the one that keeps us stuck. In fact, if you replace "of" in the preceding list of fears with "I can't handle [insert the rest of the fear]," you get a different reading. Instead of "of retribution" or "of being accountable," you get "I can't handle retribution" and "I can't handle being accountable." This new reading can be very helpful.

If you believe you have a fear of criticism, for example, you may decide to avoid situations in which you may be criticized. Then one day, you wake up wondering why you feel so confined. If you believe you have a fear of *handling* criticism, on the other hand, your search for a solution is redirected inward. You may actually begin to consider the possibility that perhaps you can indeed handle whatever criticism is necessary in order to reach a higher goal.

## Antidotes to Individual Fear

The following are two of the most effective ways to reduce our individual fear levels.

1. Recognize how we participate in lack of closure.

2. Reduce buzzing.

Let's look at these one at a time.

### *Recognize How We Participate in Lack of Closure*

When it comes time to close a communication or an issue—to agree what will be done, by when, and by whom—most of us experience some fear. It may be minimal or overpowering, but most of us spend at least a little energy wondering: Will I be able to keep the commitment? Will the other person keep their commitment? What will happen if we don't?

Sometimes these worries actually keep us from reaching closure. We're just trying to get comfortable when we avoid closure. But by participating in the lack of closure, we actually increase our level of fear and become *more* uncomfortable. We inject more uncertainty and wondering into the situation. We still don't know exactly how the issue will resolve itself—but without closure, we don't even have a proposed plan!

So the first step to minimizing fear is to look at how we may be participating in the lack of closure. Under stress, most of us experience an automatic "Them vs. Us" reaction. We want to protect ourselves. The team's problems become glaringly apparent, and so does the participation of other team members in the lack of closure. But strangely, our own participation becomes almost invisible.

Here is a list of ways people have told us that they participated in lack of closure:

- procrastinate (avoid anticipated pain)
- wait for change of leadership (in attitude and/or personnel)
- don't speak up/communicate
- give up without persisting to closure
- have hidden standards ("They should know this.")
- worry instead of acting
- test the other person instead of taking responsibility
- get sick
- leave the situation without resolution
- are not available to others
- do not have a sense of urgency
- do not take a risk to make things better
- wait for someone else to take the initiative
- become defensive
- do not listen
- lose focus
- avoid conflict
- become argumentative
- don't give input and thus don't own it
- are selective to whom they tell the truth
- play politics versus do what is needed
- play the victim or buy into being victimized
- do not spend sufficient time together
- make assumptions without checking them out
- claim, "we don't know each other well enough/haven't built trust"
- work around it versus confront the issue
- use time-zone differences as an excuse to avoid closure
- become apathetic
- participate in negative buzz

## Folk Theorem XVI.
*The best antidote to individual fear is to recognize one's own participation in lack of closure.*

The benefit of changing our participation in lack of closure is that we shift our perspective. We deal with fear not by talking it down to a less threatening emotion, but by changing the way we behave. When each of us sees our own part in the matter and becomes willing to act differently, we raise the collective level of closure in the team and create a new momentum.

We are all part of the roadblock to closure at times. Bill was the CEO of a small but successful company. He had achieved his position through hard work, long experience, and sheer force of personality. Bill overwhelmed any obstacle that arose through commitment, an abundance of energy, and sustained optimism. He had Churchill's admonition to "Never give up" etched on the inside of his mental windshield to reinforce this persistence. He was also a nice guy who cared for the people in his organization and craved their connection in return.

Bill's qualities were mostly positive, but occasionally people felt they couldn't approach him with problems or negative news. He was simply too cheery. Bill's was more than a pedestal condition; he was like a pillar of fire. Bill was left out of the loop at times when he might have been very helpful in solving problems, and these difficulties were not addressed until they had grown into crises that landed on his desk.

Fortunately, Bill was a good listener. When we began working with him and his company, he was able to hear that people wanted to tell him things but were reluctant to disturb his euphoria. He brought the team together and gave them permission—in the form of unconditional "diplomatic immunity"—to raise issues with him promptly. He then demonstrated his openness to hearing about problems in the days following the meeting, and acknowledged the courage of those who were the first to take him up on his invitation. The problem was faced head-on, and with good humor, so Bill substantially reduced the level of fear in his organization and enjoyed a new level of connection with his team.

It takes courage to recognize how we are participating in the lack of closure, and then to own that participation. It's uncomfortable. But ultimately, it becomes more satisfying than the alternatives, one of which is buzzing. Buzzing might give us a quick hit and a titillating sense of collusion, but sooner or later we see that it's interfering with our deeper urge to serve and contribute. After a steady diet of chocolate, our system craves something more nourishing.

## Reduce Buzzing

Reducing the level of buzz also diminishes fear. Buzzing is fear's Greek chorus. It magnifies problems, making them seem more dire than they may actually be. When buzzing is diminished, the energy we were wasting can be redirected to solving real problems. The beasts in the woods don't seem so big anymore.

By eliminating our own individual buzzing, we make an enormous contribution to changing the atmosphere on the team. As soon as people see the pernicious effect of buzzing and start to develop their own skills for closure, buzzing decreases naturally.

Breaking the buzzing habit also means resisting another's invitation to buzz. Understanding the difference between brainstorming and buzzing helps when you want to say "No." Brainstorming moves toward closure, while buzzing has the tone of a complaint. It is also useful to remember that the people who are trying to get you to buzz didn't set out to be destructive. They were probably just frustrated by not being able to get closure, and are acting out of habit. Hate the buzz, but love the buzzer.

What action steps can you take to eliminate buzzing? First, you can suggest that the team work together on this project. Learn to identify the various forms that buzzing takes. Then learn to interrupt the invitation to buzz early by asking what you can do to help: "Should I just listen, or would you like me to suggest solutions?" or "Are we buzzing, or are we closing?" Practice staying connected, but not agreeing with the buzz. When asked for an opinion, move the discussion to brainstorming for ways to reach closure. Pose questions about how the person intends to solve the problem, and by when. Ask to be kept informed, and set a time for your next communication. All of this helps the cause, and a winning campaign begins to take shape.

The oncology department of a large urban hospital found itself caught up in a classic "Them vs. Us" dynamic driven by recent cost-cutting mandates. Caregivers came to suspect the administration (the "money people") of personal greed, and of valuing profit before care. The administration thought the caregivers were oblivious to financial realities and accused them of indulging their "artist" mentality.

The buzz became rampant. In break rooms, otherwise competent and well-intending people spent inordinate amounts of time "trashing" the administration, greeting any attempt by the administration to increase efficiency with suspicion and automatic rejection. An unspoken agreement emerged within the oncology team: "It's useless, even disloyal, to trust the administration." All this buzzing resulted in patient and staff complaints, increased employee turnover, delays, and the failure of a community outreach program.

This got people's attention, and they decided to do something about their situation. With the intervention of a trained facilitator, team members came to see the buzzing's negative consequences to themselves and to the patients—quite apart from the administration's motives. They formulated the following guidelines for dealing with buzz—or, as they put it, "trash talk."

1. Assess the talker's intention.

2. Decide whether to listen.

3. If we decline to listen, we have the option to offer an alternative resource for listening.

4. Seek out a private area.

5. Don't fan the flames.

6. Synopsize what you heard.

7. After listening, offer choices of how you might help: to be a sounding board only, to give advice, to intervene. Ask if he or she wants your help. Encourage the parties to communicate directly.

8. Ask the talker's opinion of what he or she can do to solve the problem.

9. Ask for follow-up.

10. After closure, put it behind you. If you involved a third party, make sure he or she is aware of the closure.

The team immediately experienced a dramatic reduction in destructive buzz and a corresponding rise in real problem-solving. Buzzing became the exception rather than the unconscious rule.

## Antidotes to Organizational Fear

What people fear most about any organization is that they will be treated arbitrarily or unfairly. In the absence of rules and explicit guidelines such as those in the Trust Model, they look to the atmosphere, or what's "in the air" around the organization, for information. They make sweeping, usually inaccurate, assumptions about what is going on and how they will be treated based on nothing more than "the feel of things."

Traditionally, organizations do not manage their culture or atmosphere. Culture is not an external, objective factor—not a lever or throttle—and so managing it is more subtle than simply pushing a button. Managing an organization's culture means counting on trust, security, creativity, and connection as much as on approval levels, budgets, objectives, and internal rates of return.

The result is that we usually let the atmosphere develop randomly. That means it develops negatively. So when people don't have explicit guidelines, stick their finger up to feel the air, and make up what they *think* the atmosphere is, we usually come up with something negative. The picture is often constructed from our own blind spots. When we see a blank screen, we sometimes project onto it our own worst imaginings, suspicions, and skepticism.

The antidote, obviously, is to consciously drive a culture of trust and to give people as much information as possible about what is going on.

---

FOLK THEOREM XVII.

*If the leadership does not provide full information, the interpretations generated by the team will almost always be more pessimistic, cynical, and insidious than the truth.*

---

## Antidotes to Fear of Risk

One of the most common organizational fears is the fear of risk. Risk always brings up the possibility of failure, and that brings up fear.

The leadership of one manufacturing company had trouble when it tried to raise the level of risk-taking. We investigated, and these are some of the comments we got from high-level managers:

- "Everything is perceived as 'must be successful.'"
- "People disassociate from those who don't win."
- "The real system is one of judgment and appraisal."
- "The system has a long memory."
- "People are trained to follow the rules, not break them."
- "We have a perfectionist culture, not mistake-tolerant."

In this brooding environment, it's no wonder that getting people to take risks was difficult. To correct the situation, this company managed its atmosphere toward trust by adopting explicit guidelines for managing risk. These guidelines diminished fear by giving people a procedure to follow when they were considering risks, one that could be broken down into small, actionable steps. They defined the organization's rules around risk, so that people didn't have to carry the full burden of success or failure personally. These guidelines were also a way to improve risk management incrementally. If the outcome wasn't satisfactory, they could fix the guidelines, not the people.

This same five-step Risk Model has been used successfully by many companies we've worked with to unstick risk-taking and provide an effective way of distinguishing between sound risk and recklessness.

### The Risk Model

*Step 1: Recognize Risk.* Acknowledge the emotional content of the risk. Know that people are standing on the diving board, trying to decide whether or not to jump—and that they may be shivering. Recognize both the risks involved in taking action and the risks involved in *not* taking action. Understand and state the goal that brought up the possibility of taking this risk in the first place.

*Step 2: Assess the Risk.* List all relevant doubts and questions. Divide these into categories: answers that are known, answers for which research is required, and answers that cannot be known now, that represent an irreducible or unavoidable risk. Define the key questions and conduct the research. Determine the irreducible risk with as much specificity as possible. Determine the probability of worst-case scenarios, and decide whether or not you could survive them.

*Step 3: Choose a Path.* Determine choice points, where you will have to take one direction or another. Determine go or no-go points. Make a plan that has contingencies and a potential stopping point.

*Step 4: Build Support.* Identify your network of support. Make specific support agreements up front. Update these agreements regularly. Realign your support if it slips.

*Step 5: Make It Happen.* Own the result. Document your successes, and learn from failure by adjusting your guidelines for sound risk. Judge your results on the soundness of the risk you took. Eliminate "capricious" punishment. It's a poor substitute for effective risk management. Celebrate.

## Antidotes to Fear of Change

Change is always difficult. It brings up the possibility of loss and the feeling of being out of control. There is much that organizations can do to minimize, or even neutralize, fear that is caused by change.

Change is especially painful when we're afraid we won't be able to reach closure on something that involves "survival emotions" such as fear. Survival emotions always arise from situations involving the unknown, potential personal loss, and the fear associated with loss and the unknown. Again, lack of information is an invitation to fill in the blanks with negative assumptions. The level of negativity is usually in direct proportion to the intensity of the fear of loss.

The antidote is *information*. Where people are actually going to experience real loss—as in downsizing—it's your call when to tell them. Earlier, rather than later, is usually better in the long run.

Another antidote to fear of change is *getting people's buy-in*. The importance of buy-in increases in proportion to the degree of change. You may remember from Chapter 2 the utility company that reorganized and relocated all senior human resources (HR) personnel back to the headquarters. The result was disastrous because they never got the

HR people's buy-in. Two senior managers "couldn't find" housing in the headquarters area and continued to return home each weekend. Human resources "emergencies" arose in another site, requiring the local HR manager to delay his transition. "Them vs. Us" arguments arose between the "old guard" and recently hired new team members.

Eventually, the vice president in charge of this transition brought in professional facilitators. They conducted confidential interviews and discovered many fears: of losing customer contact, of customer anxiety over the changes, of not being able to deploy the necessary people in time, of having to turn around and decentralize again in two to three years (an acknowledged possibility). Deeper fears included displeasing the boss in times of major change, appearing not to be going along with the program, and being a "drag" on progress.

A two-day "buy-in" meeting then got down to these real issues. The team categorized doubts and fears as (1) satisfactorily addressed, (2) requiring investigation, and (3) not answerable at this time. These last were the irreducible risk for some or all of the team. The buy-in meeting began a sense of trust based on the *shared* risk of the situation.

Ultimately, the Trust Model is the antidote to organizational fear. It provides reliable guidelines for how the organization will treat its people. It reduces the fear of random or capricious behavior. A reliable promise of trust is of universal interest and appeal.

## Conditions That Influence Fear

Individual and organizational fears can be heavily influenced by conditions on the team and in the organization. Some of these conditions, and the ways to optimize them, are described in this section.

*Attitude Toward Risk.* We've seen that risk guidelines let people take sound risks without fear of retribution. The distinction between "sound risk" and "unsound risk" is subtle. With sound risk, team members have looked closely at the potential risks and benefits of the action in question, and have determined in advance that the risk is worth taking, given the potential benefits. Sound risk acknowledges the possibility of failure, but is approached with an explicitly stated "we-are-all-in-this-together" team attitude. Sound risk, managed in this way, does not allow for scapegoating. Unsound risk represents a reckless approach.

It can be avoided by making sure that all team members' doubts are fully explored and respected. When the organization gives people clear guidelines, like those in the Risk Model, the fear associated with risk is minimized.

*Penalties and Consequences for Risk That Fails.* Irrational penalties and consequences blunt a team's intelligence—both in the discussion prior to undertaking a risk and in the postmortem discussion following sound risk that fails. Intelligence includes hearing many points of view and *holding* these different points of view *simultaneously*, maintaining the tension until the right answer emerges. This requires discipline on the part of team members to stay in the tension and not bolt for comfort. They cannot give in to personal fears about the outcome. If team members penalize one another, they break ranks and stifle understanding. Risk Model guidelines should be explicit that the organization does not punish sound risk that fails.

*Permission to Disagree.* Another condition affecting fear is the organization's attitude toward disagreement. We need to be able to disagree without being "called on the carpet" simply for voicing an opposing opinion. In fact, when someone is called on the carpet for voicing a disagreement, it almost always means that the agenda of the person doing the "calling" has become more important than the team's agenda. This dynamic has no place on a connected team, because it generates fear.

---

### FOLK THEOREM XVIII.
*Disagreements are the beginning of intelligence.*

---

Disagreements are a sign that creativity is operating—and the team will figure out very quickly whether or not the leader really wants to hear dissenting views.

*Limiting Beliefs.* Over time, every team unconsciously develops beliefs that may limit its productivity. Centuries ago, the people of a seaside fishing village observed a fishing boat go out to sea, reach the horizon, and never return. The "truth" they concluded from this experience, in the midst of their loss and fear, was that the boat fell off the edge of the world. Soon people forgot the original incident and simply believed, as a habit, that the world was flat. This belief was widely held for centuries, and it imposed the limitation that people only fished within sight of the shore. That mitigated danger and reduced loss, but it limited their capacity to fish and to explore.

A set of circumstances, combined with survival-level emotions, produced an assumption that eventually became "fact." The same thing happens on teams, with the result that teams limit what is possible for them.

The corollary to this principle is that unlimited beliefs produce unlimited results. One of the reasons that certain start-ups succeed where larger companies fail is that the people running the start-ups don't know that certain ideas are considered preposterous and doomed to failure. They don't have the burden of a particular limiting belief. These people often explain later that they were too ignorant to know that their idea wouldn't work.

When IBM came out with its Selectric typewriter, Royal was the dominant supplier of office typewriters. Royal laughed at the silly "golf-ball" printing element. Surely it couldn't work, and surely IBM didn't have salespeople who knew how to sell typewriters. Royal was soon out of the typewriter business.

Teams have three kinds of limiting beliefs:

1. **What the team believes about itself.** "We've always done it this way. . . . It doesn't pay to tell the truth around here. . . . We don't have the talent to pull it off . . . We've lost our pride. . . . We need crisis. . . . If you speak up, you will be penalized. . . . We don't have the resources. . . . You have to go along to get along. . . ."

2. **What the team believes other teams think about it.** "We are considered second-class citizens. . . . We are perceived as a drag on corporate earnings. . . . We don't get any respect. . . ." One team even told us, and this is an actual quote, "We are the group on which the company performs medical experiments."

3. **What the team believes about others.** "Marketing is made up of a bunch of idiots and has all the money. . . . The human resources cops always get in the way of actually accomplishing anything. . . . MIS is incompetent. . . . Top management does not support us. . . ."

*Scapegoating.* Scapegoating can become so habitual that it becomes part of the organization's *modus operandi*. *Scapegoat* is a term invented in the sixteenth century, with roots in ancient Jewish law. One of two goats was chosen by lot and sent alive into the wilderness, with the sins of the people symbolically laid upon it, while the other was kept and sacrificed. In modern business, goats have been replaced by people. When something goes wrong, the blame is laid on the back of the scapegoat and carried off—but today that same goat is sacrificed as well!

All cases of scapegoating result from unresolved muck. The connected team understands our human tendency toward scapegoating and knows that it does not lead to solutions. Scapegoating is an indulgence that increases fear and decreases trust. The alternative to scapegoating is for the team to carry the responsibility for the situation together and find solutions from its superordinate intelligence.

**The Demon in the Company.** Very occasionally, people show up at work with a truly malicious intent. These people feed on negativity and tend to promote cynicism, conflict, and despair. It's important to resolve issues generated by these people quickly and thoroughly, because the effect of their presence on trust is dramatic. They can destroy morale and erode people's confidence in leadership to protect the team's integrity.

*Structural Defects.* Structural defects in the organization also generate fear. These include "acting" positions such as "acting president" and "acting sales manager." "Acting" can communicate reservations about the person playing the role, and it says that more change is coming—possibly accompanied by further disruption. The team keeps waiting for the other shoe to drop, and this lack of certainty is a breeding ground for fear. When a leader is labeled "acting," perhaps the rest of the team should be labeled "wondering." If you give someone a job, leave off the scarlet A.

Another type of structural defect is the "dotted-line relationship." Dotted lines on an organizational chart say, "We've almost got this figured out, but we needed to fudge something about the last step." It often has to do with not hurting someone's feelings, and the dotted line is the lifeline thrown out to rescue an ego. The cost of preserving these feelings can be doubt and worry in the team environment. People try to figure out what's really going on from the thickness of, or the percentage of white space in, the dotted line.

---

## FOLK THEOREM XIX.
*Dotted lines on an organization chart virtually always represent a failure by leadership to bite some bullet.*

---

In some cases, a dotted line attaches to a perceived "snitch" who actually reports to someone several levels above him or her on the chart. Or it may run to a "spy" assigned to a remote office to keep the home front apprised of what is really going on. This practice often occurs in multinational companies.

Other structural defects that create fear include leaving leadership positions unfilled for long periods of time, conflicting and overlapping charters, people penciled into a role who clearly don't have the time to execute it, "watchdog" positions whose sole purpose is to observe and critique others, repeated changes in leadership without explanation, constant reorganization, and the persistent use of temporary organizational structures such as "Tiger Teams."

There is no doubt that *some* of these approaches are necessary *some* of the time. But, when they are used, they need to be accompanied by clear explanations to everyone involved.

*Management by Neglect or Exclusion.* This means that critical strategic decisions are made by only one or two members of the lead team, usually the CEO and CFO, to the exclusion of other team members. This behavior is often justified by such statements as, "We can't have a democracy at the top when there is a crisis." Significant changes, even such changes as the sale of the company, are then announced suddenly to senior staff members, who thought they would have gotten to vote on such matters.

Boards of directors can also engage in this behavior, making significant decisions and surprising the lead team with their dramatic news: "We've just terminated the CEO, and in the next thirty days you will have a new owner," or "Today we just sold the XYZ Division." They often justify keeping people out of the loop for "public disclosure reasons." Senior staffers then rightly conclude that the organization is run by one or two people, and that the rest are pawns. The logical response is to disengage and abdicate any true leadership accountability.

The rest of the organization experiences an even more dramatic shift. People start looking out for themselves, not for the company. They begin thinking more about their pensions and layoff benefits than about how to contribute to the organization. A contagious victim mentality—"I can't control my career"—leads to buzzing, "Them vs. Us" politics, disassociation, pretended commitments, and general paralysis. Trust is lost, replaced by an attitude of "They don't care; why should I?" Productivity drops, performance drifts, and the leadership often appears fragmented and isolated from the employees.

*Change of Leadership.* Changes in leadership without a continued commitment to trust principles can cause major damage. The team is likely to fall back into old patterns of nonclosure and false commitments, and the organization finds it difficult to move forward.

All of these conditions that influence fear can be eliminated or minimized by applying trust principles and giving people clear guidelines for interacting with one another.

## Antidotes to Leadership Fear

People have special kinds of fears about leaders. Some of these fears stem from assumptions they make about leaders. Others have their roots in leaders' behavior. We can do something about all of these fears.

One type of "leadership fear" arises from insufficient communication. Many leaders have not had the benefit of much training in communication, so they may prefer one-on-one to team communication. This tends to create uncertainty and lack of clarity on the team—and, of course, uncertainty and lack of clarity are breeding grounds for fear. The leader may also resort to even less effective measures, such as not communicating at all.

Incomplete communication gives rise to "information holes" on such issues as the real reasons for changes in the organization, anticipated further changes, what is going on in other groups, what is expected of people, how the numbers look, and so forth. We've seen that when people don't have enough information, they fill in the holes as quickly as they can—usually with negative assumptions.

The antidote is to be aware of these information potholes and go to any lengths to communicate as openly, clearly, generously, and completely as possible.

It's also important to be aware of some automatic assumptions that people make about leaders, and not let these assumptions go unchecked or uncorrected. The most common assumption is that if leaders don't talk about their fear, it isn't there. Make sure people know that you are human and can use their support.

Another assumption is that effective leaders know what people need. This takes people off the hook. They don't have to speak up and tell the leader how to support them. They don't even have to stop and figure out what their needs *are*. That's the leader's job. If the leader doesn't support them and fulfill their needs effectively, then he or she is insensitive, or boorish, or stupid, or shows favoritism, or is prejudiced, or went to the wrong school, or drives a weird car, or is a typical male or a typical female.

Another assumption people make is that leaders are responsible for their success or failure. They hand over this responsibility to leaders without articulating their needs, defining their own vision for success, coming to terms with their own strengths and weaknesses, or calling on all of their own resources. Then they blame leaders if things don't work out.

People rarely communicate these assumptions about leaders. Instead, they set up a hidden standard and proceed to test the leader on them. The Trust Model gives people the power to eliminate hidden standards through direct and explicit communication, and the power to take their success into their own hands.

## Greed: Poisoning the Well

Greed is the cousin of fear, and requires some of the same antidotes. We define *greed* as "excessive or reprehensible acquisitiveness." There is no faster way to kill a team's spirit and productivity than for the leadership to act out of its own greed. The fear this generates is enormous, and in many cases justified.

Since greed is the engine that drives our economy, we often see the people who are the most acquisitive and driven at the top of companies. When power and money are the primary motivation for rising in the ranks, we sometimes end up with leaders shrewd in the ways of acquiring power and money but little else. Worse, if the power impulse is rooted in a personal insecurity or fear, we wind up with the inmates running the asylum.

***Greed, Fear, and Ego.*** Greed often has its roots in fear. When this is the case, we think, "I am not happy now, but acquiring this thing will take away my fear and insecurities." Then we get afraid we won't be able to acquire that thing.

In other cases, greed grows out of a sense of scarcity, a hoarding mentality that there is not enough money, love, faith, success, good men, good women, or whatever to go around—that these things are scarce and hard to find.

*Ego*, as the word is commonly used, is a form of greed as well. We feel threatened and try to defend ourselves with image management, an invented persona, dominance, prevarication, or repression. Ego goes about acquiring what it thinks it needs to protect itself, secretly believing that "what is good for me is good for General Motors"—that if my ego gets satisfied, it'll be good for everyone.

The team knows intuitively that this is not the case. They understand that by trying to support both the leader's ego needs and the team's results, they are attempting to serve two masters. A more productive strategy is for leaders to let themselves be vulnerable and communicate their authentic doubt or confusion so that the team can help.

Another challenge is that ego never wants to admit being wrong. If the captain of a ship discovers he has been steering in the wrong direction, he may be reluctant to make the necessary course correction immediately—but he usually does because of the dire consequences of continuing in the wrong direction. We expect our organizational captains to make those corrections, but sometimes it seems that they are willing to run aground rather than accept the need to change. We find out too late that, rather than keeping watch out the window of the steering house, they have been gazing in the mirror.

We have seen companies that were held together by nothing but shared greed, and it was not a pretty sight. At the first sign of economic downturn or disappointment, the centripetal forces that were already in place tore these organizations apart. Conversely, we have seen organizations go through the toughest of economic times intact when they were connected by principles of trust.

Greed is a universal impulse, and we are all subject to its call at one time or another. It's useless to deny greed and pretend that our business organizations are charitable institutions. The bottom line is still the bottom line, and profitability is the fuel for the engine of the enterprise. The productive strategy is to look greed in the eye and deal with it using trust principles.

***Hubris.*** Hubris is overweaning pride or self-confidence, and often appears in Greek mythology as a fatal flaw in character. Hubris is a form of greed. When Icarus discovered that he could fly using wings held together with wax, he succumbed to pride and soared too close to the sun despite his father's warnings. The wax melted and he fell to his death.

Hubris often comes into play just as companies start to achieve success. They begin to believe that if they can do one thing well, they can do anything well. When this turns out to be false, as it often does, the company finds itself in over its head.

One successful high-tech company focused its early efforts on building certain system components, always ensuring that it had the highest quality and most advanced designs in the industry. It grew rapidly, went public, and made a fortune for the founders. The management team then decided to go into systems *and* associated software—a much different business from the business of providing components. They reasoned that the expansion was a good idea because this was a high-growth field, but the real engine behind their decision was hubris. Their early success had given them an exaggerated view of their own capability, which turned out to be disastrous.

***Hoarding.*** Hoarding occurs wherever there is perceived scarcity, and it can be just as destructive to trust as overt greed. Hoarding on teams usually takes the form of keeping secrets, withholding information, or not giving recognition or acknowledgment.

The root of *recognition* is to "know again." Recognition means having your contributions openly acknowledged and "known again" by the team. It registers your success and confirms your competence and value. When recognition is withheld, the team becomes disconnected.

*Temptation.* Fear and greed can begin to feed on themselves. We have seen more than one company culture shift from high-minded ideals of service and integrity to deceit, manipulation, and exploitation under leadership changes or financial stress. It takes great skill to hold a company together during difficult transitions, and there is always a temptation to jettison principles in favor of other expedients. Leadership that takes this path may survive temporarily, but a better investment is to preserve the integrity, intelligence, and values of the team. That is what creates the greatest success over time.

## Overcoming Fear and Greed

In a leadership organization, ongoing fear and greed have no constructive role. People shrink in the presence of these conditions, and the team regresses to a collection of individual members working parallel to one another, not synergistically. The exponential effect of team connection is lost. You can tell this downward spiral has begun when people start to look out for themselves and no longer notice whether or not their teammates are winning.

Our experience with a West Coast company shows what happens when fear and greed come together and take over an organization. The visionary founder of this company had successfully launched a series of specialized conferences for the high-tech industry. These conferences had grabbed everyone's attention and came to dominate the field. Giddy with this early success, the founding team started considering options for expansion. Two paths were identified. One was to sponsor conferences in other geographical locations and increase their frequency. The other was to diversify into other modes of delivering the company's core expertise: seminars, tutorials, books, tapes, and interactive learning. They already had everything they needed to expand geographically, but they would need to acquire a whole new range of people and skills to diversify into other modes of delivery. But what the heck, they figured, why not go for it all? So they did. Or at least they tried.

The result was chaos. People felt stressed as they attempted to work in areas where they had relatively little competence. Experts in the new fields were hired quickly but integrated slowly. "Old guard vs. new guard" tensions arose. Energy at the company increased, but so did confusion, soft commitments, dropped balls, and trouble among the original principals.

Realizing that they were about to become a classic case of failure due to unfocused expansion, they stopped and took a hard look. They quickly saw that fear was driving their rush to premature expansion— fear of letting someone else grab the business, of being upstaged, of falling behind, and also fear of boredom, of being stuck in the repetitive business of running conferences over and over again, repeating a formula rather than inventing new ones. They also saw that greed was unconsciously pushing them in the wrong direction. Lack of focus can often be traced to greed, to the impulse to grab as much as you can, while you can.

The team made some critical decisions about risk. They saw that doing more of what they already knew—more conferences in more locations—was the sound risk choice for them at that time. Expanding into what they didn't know—different modes of delivery—entailed unnecessary and even reckless risk.

They changed their path back to geographic expansion, and their resulting success is legendary in the industry. Combined attendance at their conferences rose from a few thousand to over one hundred thousand in less than five years, and is still increasing. They now hold conferences all over the world. The market value of this "dull, repetitive, boring conference business" is measured in hundreds of millions of dollars, giving the company the economic freedom to look for other ways to innovate outside the original business.

Organizations spend enormous amounts of time and money on traditional exercises such as reorganizing, writing mission statements, and defining values—only to wake up months or years later and discover that nothing has changed. This is often because they have not gotten to the heart of the matter. They have not understood how muck, fear, and greed are impacting the team, or how these dynamics became so widespread. And they haven't understood how simply and effectively the Trust Model can act as an antidote.

In the next five chapters, you will see exactly how to create and implement a Trust Model designed specifically for your organization, and how to make it work each day for the people in your organization.

# Part IV

# IMPLEMENTING THE TRUST MODEL

# 8

# Phase 1: Commit the Leadership

How DO YOU actually go about creating an organizational culture based on trust, so that you can enjoy the benefits of increased productivity, profits, and satisfaction? The next five chapters take you step-by-step through the five phases of developing, implementing, and maintaining Trust Model guidelines that promote this culture.

## The Five Phases of Implementing Trust

The Trust Model process—creation, buy-in, and maintenance of your organizational trust guidelines—is the foundation of your trust culture. To optimize your benefits, we recommend that you use these five specific phases for building and maintaining your trust guidelines:

1. Commit the leadership.

2. Assess the level of trust and closure in your organization. (This phase is optional.)

3. Formulate your Trust Model guidelines.

4. Commit the organization.

5. Maintain your Trust Model.

The time it takes to complete each phase depends on the size of your organization, the level of commitment to the process, and the amount of muck that has accumulated on your team. In almost every case, you can realize some benefit in a matter of days or weeks, and these benefits multiply over time. The Trust Model is a little like a sport in which you master the basic movement quickly and then spend a lifetime refining and improving your skill.

For each of the five phases, we will describe the objectives and issues that are likely to arise. We are not suggesting that there is only one way to accomplish each phase. Quite the contrary. Placing trust at the center of organizational culture is new territory, and there is a great deal of opportunity for you to innovate and tailor your guidelines to your particular organization. You may come up with ideas and possibilities that haven't occurred to us or to any of the groups with which we've worked, and these new methods may be the perfect solution for your team.

## Three Warnings to Leaders

Trust is powerful stuff, and we offer three caveats before you embark on this path.

1. **The road to trust is actually a one-way street.** Once you start out on the journey toward trust in your organization, we advise you not to turn back. Trust is serious business and strikes a deep chord in people. If you announce that you are going to run the organization based on trust, and then later change your mind and try something else, people will not like it. In fact, they may become very upset. This is a genie you can't put back into the bottle.

2. **In choosing the Trust Model, you commit not just to developing and implementing your trust guidelines, but also to maintaining them.** You are in it for the long term, so it's best to deal up front with any doubts or fears you have about the Trust Model, or about putting trust at the center of your organizational culture. Anything that's worrying you or holding you back is likely to be mirrored in your team—so confront your own fears or trepidations first, before talking to the rest of the team. You'll be in a better position to win their buy-in if you've handled your own doubts first.

3. **Starting to implement the Trust Model will release energy in your organization and generate a reaction.** Remember that any negative or volatile reaction people may have is mostly a response to their own fears, and not about you personally. Give them permission to communicate specifically and overtly, so that their reactions don't go underground and fester. In most cases, the reaction will be respectful—but even when it isn't, you'll need to encourage more communication, not less.

# The Objective of Phase 1

The objective of this phase is to present the concept of the Trust Model to the lead team as a way of building organizational trust, and to gain their commitment and buy-in. The lead team needs to get behind the Trust Model, to own it as the vehicle carrying your organization toward a trust-based culture, and to become personally responsible for its success. For some people, trust principles will be new and possibly even challenging. Regardless of their reaction, your job is to keep modeling trust and to encourage communication.

Leaders commit to the Trust Model for a variety of reasons. In one case, the new general manager of a 300-person product division heard consistent feedback that her lead team mistrusted just about everything that happened in the company. The situation demanded a bold stroke, and she chose the Trust Model to make it. In one start-up company, the Trust Model was considered the best way to build a high-performance culture. In a third company, the leader simply got fed up with the squabbling and "Them vs. Us" dynamics associated with their high level of nonclosure. The Trust Model is also an excellent way to bring together corporate cultures and create trust after a merger or acquisition.

So the first question for your lead team is this: Even though you may experience some personal discomfort, are the benefits that you hope to gain from the Trust Model worth the effort? If the lead team answers "Yes" to this question, they are saying that they will be the ones who are accountable to the organization for building trust. They will need to "walk the talk," sometimes in an exaggerated way, so that people get the message.

## The Five Steps of Phase 1

The five steps you take to get your lead team's buy-in are the same that they will take later with the organization as a whole:

1. Articulate the benefits.

2. Determine the starting point.

3. Create a schedule.

4. Elicit agreement.

5. Confront doubts and fears.

The first step is to articulate the benefits of building a trust-based culture for your particular team, at this particular time. This approach brings the trust principles to life in a way that is meaningful for your lead team. Speak about how the principles can have a positive impact on specific situations in your organization. Perhaps the organization has a history of marketing and engineering not being able to get on the same page. Perhaps there is slippage in product delivery. Perhaps a remote office is feeling detached from the home organization. Perhaps the marketplace is revealing a new need for competitive advantage. In any case, put the case for trust into language that speaks directly to your team. Present it as a solution to specific problems that everyone understands. Ask if everyone agrees, and elicit their examples of how it might work.

Second, determine a starting point for your Trust Model process. You may be ready to implement the Trust Model across your entire organization right away, or you may want to start with a pilot team. If you take this latter route, we suggest you choose a pilot team that touches as many other areas of the organization as possible—management information systems or finance, for example—so that people can see the benefits of trust-based teamwork firsthand.

Third, create a schedule for going from Phase 2 through Phase 5. Develop a timeline of events and milestones that takes you systematically through the five phases of implementation: committing the lead team, assessing the level of trust and closure in your organization, formulating your Trust Model guidelines, committing the organization, and maintenance. Allow enough time to complete each phase fully and with ease. Don't promise too much progress too quickly. Setting a realistic schedule helps you avoid pretended commitments.

Fourth, elicit agreement from the team. Make sure everyone has a chance to air their views, and then ask for buy-in.

Fifth, uncover and confront any doubts and fears that people may have. This is critical. If people don't have a chance to consider their doubts, voice their questions and concerns, and be heard, all those doubts and fears will stay beneath the surface and their commitment may be halfhearted or pretended. If this is the case, the process will bog down later. It's easier and more efficient to deal with all the doubts and fears up front.

When you elicit the team's doubts and fears, they usually fall into three categories:

1. **Those to which the team already knows the answer.** These include whether or not people feel that trust is an issue, what their own level of interest is, how much time is available for a new initiative, etc.

2. **Those for which the team can get answers.** These include whether or not the rest of the staff feels trust is an issue, how customers or partners feel about the company, how much time all of this trust-building will take, etc.

3. **Those that the team cannot answer now.** These include whether or not the workload will change dramatically in an atmosphere of trust, whether or not the leader will go through a personality transformation, etc.

The team can find answers for the first two categories of questions, and then determine whether the irreducible risk associated with the third kind is acceptable and sound or reckless and possibly fatal.

At a large management consulting firm headed by our client Janet, the lead team had these doubts about implementing a trust-based culture:

- The benefits were not obvious.
- The team would not stick with the program.
- Certain members of the team would never get on board.
- It would take too much time in a busy schedule.

Be patient and provide answers for each concern. Janet first reiterated the benefits in terms of dollars and cents, then talked about how being a trust-based organization could reduce some of the specific frustrations the team was feeling. Next, she talked about ways to stick with the program once the Trust Model guidelines were defined. For instance, they would have monthly two-hour progress meetings. She said that since she herself was already committed to following these principles, there was a good chance that others would stick with them as well. She had private discussions with the potential "problem" members of the team, obtained their support, and then had them announce their commitment to the entire team.

Finally, Janet quantified the time involved in order to address the "busy schedule" issue. She did not minimize the time required for maintenance, but challenged the team to "keep this issue in front of us so we can keep focusing on it." She showed that the time involved was actually a minor investment compared to many other initiatives already in place, and then talked about the amount of time that could be *saved* by this approach. She knew that fear of change is sometimes cloaked in "time" concerns, and wisely addressed both. She reassured people that this was not the cover for a major company upheaval, that everyone was secure in their present positions, and that they would participate in decisions affecting this new approach.

Committing your lead team is the foundation for implementing your Trust Model. Any time and energy you invest here is well worth it. Everything else you do rests on the commitment of the lead team.

Here is what Phase 1 looked like at Startup, Inc., and Bigger, Inc.

## Phase 1 at Startup, Inc.

At Startup, the lead team consisted of Randy, the CEO, and Damon and Trevor, the founders. Because Randy had some experience with trust principles and was himself completely committed, he made an excellent presentation to Damon and Trevor. After suggesting a starting point and proposing the schedule, he asked for their buy-in.

Neither Damon nor Trevor had ever worked in an environment of earned trust. On the one hand, it sounded wonderful. On the other hand, they couldn't imagine it actually happening.

"It sounds great," Damon said, "but what about when the production people don't meet deadlines and we can't get the product to customers on time?"

Randy explained that they might consider making one of their guidelines "We will make no pretended commitments" and include a policy that dealt with slippage.

Trevor asked how they would avoid pretended commitments to customers "when Damon promises them the moon and then we have to run around in circles trying to make it happen." Randy said that they might consider a guideline about getting internal agreement before they spoke to customers or vendors.

In the end, Damon and Trevor agreed to take the leap—but not before Randy had spent a couple hours answering their questions and calming their fears.

## Phase 1 at Bigger, Inc.

The lead team at Bigger included Jan, Pat, Alex, Ted, Max, Randy, and Sheryl. Sam, the CEO, wisely had this meeting facilitated by someone from the outside.

Trust was not an easy thing for this group, but they were all at the end of their ropes. They were involved in interactions that became less productive and less pleasant by the day, and they were ready to try just about anything. Sam was able to step outside of his part in "Them vs. Us" and be gracious and acknowledging enough to members of the other faction that they could hear what he said.

When he articulated the benefits of a trust-based culture and gave examples of other companies that had implemented the Trust Model with great success, people were ready to listen. It was clear that lack of trust was having a demoralizing effect on everyone and a disastrous effect on growth and profits. What Sam said made sense to the rest of the team. When he laid out a starting date and schedule, it began to seem real. There were a lot of questions about "enforcement," and the third-party facilitator had to step in from time to time, but everybody was finally satisfied that the Trust Model was worth a sincere effort.

The lead team's buy-in was the first time they had operated as a unit in almost a year.

Committing the leadership is your critical first step, the basis of your implementation. You have completed Phase 1, and now you can go forward to Phase 2.

# 9

# Phase 2: Assess the Level of Trust and Closure

ONCE YOU HAVE buy-in from the lead team, you are ready to move forward. For some organizations, it's a good idea to pause at this point and assess the current level of trust and closure in your organization. We stress that *this phase is optional*. If you don't feel a need to assess the level of trust and closure in your organization, go directly to Phase 3 (Chapter 10).

This assessment is a good idea if:

1. People have some doubt that they can actually improve trust and closure, and this doubt is keeping them from buying in completely. Their doubt might be either that trust and closure are not real problems in your organization, or that they are problems but that nothing can be done about them.

2. You want a more complete characterization of the level of trust, so that you can see how best to address it.

3. You want a quantitative benchmark, so that you have a basis for measuring improvement.

## How Do You Assess Trust?

To assess trust, Learning Center, Inc., has developed the Trust and Closure Audit Questionnaire, a set of twenty-one questions that can be asked of everyone in your organization—anonymously, if you prefer— and easily quantified. This questionnaire is particularly powerful because it is designed to detect both the overall level of trust and the types of issues in which closure is a concern.

You can process the data from the questionnaire results in many ways. Obviously, it will tell you the level of trust in your organization, but you can also determine the level of trust in each department or by type of issue. If you repeat the test over time, you can determine trends in the level of trust.

This questionnaire is one of many ways to measure trust. You know best which method will work for you. If you feel that a questionnaire might not work for your team, you might begin by soliciting anonymous responses to such open-ended questions as:

- Do you feel this is a trustworthy team that reaches closure consistently? Why or why not?
- How satisfied are you with your work relationships, including with your boss, peer group, and other associates?
- Why are your best working relationships as good as they are? What are the factors that help make them so good?
- How do you think some of your work relationships could be improved?
- What are a few of the things you like about working here?
- Are there any changes you would like to suggest that would make this a better place to work?

You might also hold confidential one-on-one interviews to find out what people are thinking.

## Trust and Closure Audit Questionnaire

1. If our organization was suddenly forced into a painful change of unknown dimension, I'm confident that significant proportions of our workplace would communicate their concerns and seek ways to help.

   ☐ Strongly Agree  ☐ Agree  ☐ Neutral  ☐ Disagree  ☐ Strongly Disagree

2. I can honestly say that 80 percent or more of our communications close immediately in some form.

   ☐ Strongly Agree  ☐ Agree  ☐ Neutral  ☐ Disagree  ☐ Strongly Disagree

3. I am confident that my organization is not encouraging risk-averse behavior.

   ☐ Strongly Agree  ☐ Agree  ☐ Neutral  ☐ Disagree  ☐ Strongly Disagree

4. If I were troubled by an impending change, real or rumored, I could safely confide my concerns and seek solutions with my immediate manager or board.

   ☐ Strongly Agree  ☐ Agree  ☐ Neutral  ☐ Disagree  ☐ Strongly Disagree

5. Conflict is handled openly and resolved in a timely manner.

   ☐ Strongly Agree  ☐ Agree  ☐ Neutral  ☐ Disagree  ☐ Strongly Disagree

6. Managers/teams create projects that contain clearly understood goals, plans with specific accountabilities, and intermediate milestones for progress.

   ☐ Strongly Agree  ☐ Agree  ☐ Neutral  ☐ Disagree  ☐ Strongly Disagree

7. Teams within the company consistently create an atmosphere of mutual trust and closure.

   ☐ Strongly Agree  ☐ Agree  ☐ Neutral  ☐ Disagree  ☐ Strongly Disagree

8. Cross-functional communication is efficient and results in few delays.

   ☐ Strongly Agree  ☐ Agree  ☐ Neutral  ☐ Disagree  ☐ Strongly Disagree

9. Teams consistently cultivate and harvest a "what we can learn" attitude when things do not go as expected.

   ☐ Strongly Agree  ☐ Agree  ☐ Neutral  ☐ Disagree  ☐ Strongly Disagree

10. I believe that "Them vs. Us" dynamics, within our organization and with our customers, cost us less than 2 percent of our gross revenue.

    ☐ Strongly Agree  ☐ Agree  ☐ Neutral  ☐ Disagree  ☐ Strongly Disagree

11. The majority of our workforce has a clear sense of direction and priority.

☐ Strongly Agree ☐ Agree ☐ Neutral ☐ Disagree ☐ Strongly Disagree

12. Our people know that when someone on the team says they are going to do something, they can count on it being done.

☐ Strongly Agree ☐ Agree ☐ Neutral ☐ Disagree ☐ Strongly Disagree

13. I am reasonably sure that no one on my immediate team harbors resentment or serious unspoken disagreement with me.

☐ Strongly Agree ☐ Agree ☐ Neutral ☐ Disagree ☐ Strongly Disagree

14. Our senior management fully and visibly shares the risks of painful change with the entire organization.

☐ Strongly Agree ☐ Agree ☐ Neutral ☐ Disagree ☐ Strongly Disagree

15. I consider myself a good listener, and improving.

☐ Strongly Agree ☐ Agree ☐ Neutral ☐ Disagree ☐ Strongly Disagree

16. Leadership does a good job of "walking the talk" on key organizational values.

☐ Strongly Agree ☐ Agree ☐ Neutral ☐ Disagree ☐ Strongly Disagree

17. We do a good job of recognizing both individual and team contributions.

☐ Strongly Agree ☐ Agree ☐ Neutral ☐ Disagree ☐ Strongly Disagree

18. We do a good job of addressing marginal performance and bringing these issues to closure.

☐ Strongly Agree ☐ Agree ☐ Neutral ☐ Disagree ☐ Strongly Disagree

19. Most projects/orders get done to the customer's satisfaction and on time.

☐ Strongly Agree ☐ Agree ☐ Neutral ☐ Disagree ☐ Strongly Disagree

20. Team or work group objectives are clearly aligned to the objectives of the whole organization.

☐ Strongly Agree ☐ Agree ☐ Neutral ☐ Disagree ☐ Strongly Disagree

21. I am aware that this type of assessment represents a 100 percent positive opportunity for me, for our senior management, for our workforce, and for our customers.

☐ Strongly Agree ☐ Agree ☐ Neutral ☐ Disagree ☐ Strongly Disagree

## Be Open to the Results

Be open to whatever is revealed in this questionnaire. Don't take any negative answers personally. Remember that you are just collecting information. Use that information to your advantage. Knowing where the trouble spots are gives you the best chance of dealing with them effectively.

You'll start doing that in Phase 3 of implementation: "Formulate Your Trust Model."

# 10

# Phase 3: Formulate Your Trust Model

IN THIS PHASE, the lead team actually puts together Trust Model guidelines. You design these guidelines to reflect your organization's values and needs, to give people direction as they interact with one another and go about their work, and to build a culture of trust in your organization.

Unanimity is not essential. Not everyone has to agree on every word of the Trust Model guidelines. They just need to agree to get behind them and support them. We make a distinction, as always, between agreeing with every detail of the guidelines and agreeing to proceed based on the principles the team develops. Again, you may want to invite a professional facilitator to support you and the team in this process.

There are three steps in Phase 3:

1. Review trust concepts.

2. Resolve open issues.

3. Draft your Trust Model guidelines.

## Step 1: Review Trust Concepts

The objectives of Step 1 are to deepen the lead team's understanding of the Trust Model and to prepare them to draft the guidelines. This step culminates in a meeting of the lead team to discuss essential trust concepts. Step 1 works best when you do the following:

1. Ask each member of the lead team to read this book so that they can all discuss it together at the group meeting. Point out key ideas such as the definitions of trust, closure, commitment, "Them vs. Us," muck, risk, etc.

2. Have each member of the lead team complete the following "Trust: Ten Questions for Leaders" action-plan form, and prepare to discuss their insights at the meeting.

## Trust: Ten Questions for Leaders

1. Identify any currently unresolved pretended or "soft" commitments you have made. Please complete your list before going on.

2. Circle the most important one to study and resolve.

3. Why did you make this commitment? How have you justified it in your mind? Please be very thorough.

4. If you have more than one soft commitment listed under question 1, are any of these justified in the same or similar manner? Which?

5. Regardless of the justifications under question 4, have negative consequences accrued around your circled example above? If so, what? Interpersonal consequences? Productivity consequences?

6. Are there actions on your part that might initiate resolution? If so, list them.

7. If communication is part of your strategy under question #6, how would you initiate communication? What words would you use? When?

8. List below any other currently unresolved soft commitments for which you will initiate resolution, and by when. Real commitments, please.

9. How are soft commitments affecting our organization?

10. What might you do to build a culture based on 100 percent real commitment? How might you open communication on this subject, starting today?

When the lead team looks to their own part in the situation, they begin to see how their actions have made for more trust, or less trust, within the organization. Everybody considers how they have participated in the problem, and so they are less fearful and more willing to reach closure.

3. Have the lead team review the following "Ten Leader Tips for Building Trust." This is a summary of techniques for enhancing trust on teams.

### *Ten Leader Tips for Building Trust*

1. **To build mistrust:** Complain to others about problems you are having with a peer, without attempting to solve the problem through direct communication. Establish an atmosphere where this is tolerated.
   **To build trust:** Be an effective model by solving problems through direct communication at the lowest equivalent level—yourself and peers; yourself and your direct manager; yourself, your manager, and his or her manager. Establish an atmosphere where this is the culture.

2. **To build mistrust:** Take credit for yourself, or allow others to give you credit for an accomplishment that was not all yours.

   **To build trust:** Share credit genuinely. When in doubt, share.

3. **To build mistrust:** Make a pretended or "halfhearted" commitment, e.g., "I'll get back to you."
   **To build trust:** When in doubt about taking on a commitment, air your concerns with the relevant parties. When engaged in an ongoing commitment, communicate anticipated slippage as soon as you suspect it. Ask for help.

4. **To build mistrust:** Manage/supervise/direct from behind your desk only.

To build trust: Spend "informed" time mingling, asking nonassumptive questions, and making only promises you can keep, while working back through lines of authority.

5. To build mistrust: Be unclear or not exactly explicit about what you need or expect. Assume that your subordinates "should" know without being told.
   To build trust: Be explicit and direct. Welcome questions and respond with closure.

6. To build mistrust: Withhold potentially useful opinions until the drama heightens, thus minimizing your risk of being wrong.
   To build trust: Courage means having fear and acting positively anyway. Be timely; be willing to be wrong.

7. To build mistrust: Communicate with undue abruptness when others venture new opinions or questions. Aim to have your point of view prevail.
   To build trust: Listen carefully; assign yourself to understand. Address the issue with your honest opinion. Communicate for clarity and closure.

8. To build mistrust: Create the appearance of working through an entire lead team, while actually confiding in only one or two members, or in no one at all.
   To build trust: Establish trust with all members of your lead team. Let competence and jurisdiction determine the level of your confidence.

9. To build mistrust: Hold in your mind another department's productivity or behavior as a reason for less cooperation, or for your department's shortcomings.
   To build trust: Establish direct, respectful communication, airing your problem and seeking win-win closure.

10. To build mistrust: Have performance review time the only time for coaching input.
    To build trust: Schedule regular contact for input and feedback. Develop systems for staff members to communicate specific needs for improvement to management.

4. Call a meeting of the lead team to review the first three steps and to discuss any insights, questions, variations, or elaborations they've seen. This entire process can take as little as two hours of staff time. The outcome will be (1) a common understanding of essential trust concepts, (2) a common vocabulary, and (3) people beginning to internalize these concepts and vocabulary by relating them to the specific issues on the lead team.

When your lead team has taken these four steps, each team member brings a higher level of understanding into the Trust Model process and is ready to take the next step.

## Step 2: Resolve Open Issues

Before you can move forward, you must deal with any issues that are still open or unresolved for the lead team. Where there are unresolved issues, there is muck. And as we saw in Folk Theorem X, it is impossible to trust fully while you are still in the muck. To establish trust on your team, you must first handle open issues and unresolved muck.

Again, there are four steps:

1. The leader asks everyone on the lead team to submit a list of unresolved issues. These lists can be anonymous, and can be sent to a neutral point such as a trusted administrative support person. The neutral person tabulates the lists and distributes them for resolution. As the leader, you make it clear that *all* issues will be put on the table and included in the final list. There will be no filtering or exceptions. This exercise will probably bring to the surface issues that have not yet been discussed openly, but some of the tougher issues may remain submerged. That's okay. Simply starting to peel away the layers of the onion is enough for now. It's not realistic to expect to get through all the layers in one pass.

2. Review the results of the trust and closure assessment that you did in implementation Phase 2, if this option was selected. Presumably, there will be strong correlation between the list of issues generated from the questionnaire and the list of issues submitted by the lead team. If there is significant divergence between the lead team's input

and the broader, organization-wide trust assessment, this needs to be addressed.

3. Meet to discuss these open issues. Because information has been gathered so recently, in an open environment that encourages people to tell the truth, the issues they take on will be real, important, and current. It is crucial that the team's approach be nonintrusive, validating, and self-discovering. It may be necessary to follow up this meeting with a number of one-on-one sessions with people outside the lead team—for instance, with key customers. If this is the case, the lead team should keep a master list of issues, names of people handling them, and dates for resolution. As the lead team does its work, it is practicing closure and authentic commitment.

4. Continue to meet and to practice trust principles such as closure, genuine commitments, acknowledgment of success, dealing with slippage, identifying losses, and developing remedial plans. These meetings could be the first of monthly maintenance meetings.

As you go about these four steps, be open to acknowledging the organization's history and identifying any limiting beliefs that surface. Both of these factors are part of closing open issues.

## Acknowledge History

Another part of closing open issues is to acknowledge history. If your organization's history has been particularly uncomfortable or difficult, now is the time to say so out loud—and without finger-pointing. Just hearing the truth of the situation brings many people relief and builds confidence in the process. This is definitely not the time to fudge, spin, or be defensive. Some topics that may need to be addressed are lack of direction, poor communication, promises not kept, poor change management, leadership vacuums, perceived losses (personal or organizational—from downsizing, loss of status, etc.), and disagreements. All these things create a history of mistrust.

## Identify Limiting Beliefs

This is also a good time to identify limiting beliefs the team may have about itself, other teams or departments with which it interacts, or the organization as a whole.

One medium-size high-tech manufacturing company in the Silicon Valley was losing its competitive edge despite streamlining after a purchase from the original Japanese owners. After more than a year of structural changes and low payoff, the leadership began looking at its people dynamics. First, they acknowledged history, identifying some residual "Them vs. Us" issues left over from the previous ownership. These included old "political" loyalties, insufficient communication and closure across extended time zones, and "old guard vs. new guard" divisiveness. They dealt with these through one-on-one meetings (as described in Chapter 6: "The Seven Steps to Closure"), mostly among lead-team members.

The focus then shifted to limiting beliefs. In a two-hour discussion, the team was able to identify three previously unrecognized limiting beliefs that, in fact, had a stranglehold on the company and were keeping it from being competitive:

1. A subtle *Field of Dreams*-like expectation: "If we build it, they will come." They were stuck in the limiting belief that all they had to do was have a great product and the world would make its way to their doorstep without them lifting a finger in the marketing arena. This subtle mind-set reinforced their long tradition of having such a great technical product that they never had to do much beyond some mediocre marketing. They saw that in order to hold and increase their market share now, they would have to abandon this cherished belief and do something about marketing.

2. A belief that the markets provided by their previous overseas owners were now irretrievably lost. The unspoken, but deeply held, belief was that they did not have the wherewithal to replace these markets, and their sense of helplessness left them immobilized.

3. A belief that the parts of the company that had been acquired could not be trusted and had to be tightly controlled. This belief led to stultifying actions on the part of management. It was no wonder that the high-spirited initiative necessary for creating a winning organization had disappeared.

These insights brought a universal "Aha!" from the lead team. They set about articulating and deploying Trust Model guidelines designed to encourage the rest of the organization to keep unearthing these kinds of limiting beliefs over time. The company eventually overcame its self-imposed limits. They strengthened their marketing and sales capability, found substitute markets to replace those lost in the sale of the company, and created multiple profit centers that ran on a foundation of accountability and trust. Their market penetration accelerated over the next several years, and the business began to flourish.

Unearthing unspoken emotional dynamics and limiting beliefs extends your organization's strategic capability. Rational business tools such as reorganization and distribution strategies are crucial, but the emotional perceptions of team members can be just as important. These emotional energies can be cleared, redirected, and used to form a richer and higher order of intelligence.

# Step 3: Draft Your Trust Model Guidelines

In this step, you actually set pen to paper, or fingers to keyboard, and create a draft of your Trust Model. The leader asks lead-team members to submit in writing the guidelines that they think ought to be explicitly included, and to assign a priority to each guideline. The team then meets to discuss this input, and each member has an opportunity to be heard. Then the leader, or a designated member of the team, goes off to draft the actual document and brings it back to the next session for final agreement.

## *Levels of Accountability*

In putting together this document, one thing the team should consider is how much accountability everyone in the organization will assume. For instance, the lead team must make promises to one another and to the organization for which they will be accountable. But how much accountability will they ask in return from other members of the organization? Here are some possible levels of accountability:

1. promises the lead-team members make to one another

2. promises the lead team makes to the entire organization, and does not ask the organization to make in return

3. promises the lead team makes to the organization, and wishes all employees to make to each other after buy-in and adjustments

4. promises that all employees make to each other, to customers, and possibly to other stakeholders

It is possible to start with the lead team making most of the promises—to one another and/or to the organization—and to progress incrementally to greater accountability on the part of all employees. But ultimately, you will need to get at least to option 3 in order to gain the maximum advantage of using the Trust Model. Option 4 presents a powerful approach to creating strong partnerships with customers, since the Trust Model embodies commitments that most customers only dream of. In fact, extending the Trust Model commitments to all stakeholders—suppliers, customers, partners, investors, boards of directors, etc.—creates an extended trust community that becomes tremendously powerful.

## *Subjects to Cover*

You will certainly want to cover the areas of growth and profitability. Where are you headed and why? What exactly do you want to achieve? You may also want to cover some of the other areas discussed in this book, many of which are described in Chapter 2:

- *Growth and productivity.*
- *Closure.* Close all communications.
- *Commitment.* Avoid false commitments.
- *Communication.* Use direct and open communication.
- *Speedy Resolution.* Clear up unresolved issues as soon as possible.
- *Respect.* Use tact and respect in communications.
- *Responsibility.* Own your own problems, but be willing to give and receive help.

Other topics should speak to the issues and dynamics that are particularly important to your organization. These might include such principles as how to handle risk, how to make decisions, what empowerment means and how it will be implemented, how mistakes will be handled, responsiveness, information sharing, and specific communication guidelines.

Your Trust Model guidelines should emphasize solutions to problems that have been identified in Steps 1 and 2 of Phase 3 (Chapter

10). If the team has had trouble responding to communications in a timely way, for instance, your guidelines may feature a twenty-four-hour response guideline. If silence and "stuffing" have been difficulties, your guidelines may encourage expression. One company had an eight-hundred-pound gorilla sitting in the living room in the form of a founder who misbehaved by having backdoor conversations, manipulating people, and going to the press if he did not agree with internal decisions. Their Trust Model guidelines included explicit and dire consequences for management who did not follow the rules and act as role models. If you expect a flood, get flood insurance.

## The Question of Risk

The question of how to handle risk inevitably arises when organizations formulate their Trust Model guidelines. As you look at how to approach the idea of risk in your guidelines, you may want to review Chapter 7, "Antidotes to Fear," in which we discuss risk at length.

A certain amount of risk is necessary in business. If we never risked, we would never innovate or enter the new territories that yield rich rewards. But we want to avoid uncontrollable risk, or what we call "irreducible risk," as much as possible. Often we feel as if we're standing on a diving board, weighing the pros and cons of jumping. There could be danger in going off the board, but there could be just as much danger in *not* jumping—especially in business, an arena in which missed opportunities can mean failure.

We saw in Phase 1 (Chapter 8) that when people weigh the pros and cons of committing to the Trust Model, three kinds of questions emerge:

1. Those to which we already know the answer

2. Those for which we can get answers

3. Those that we cannot answer now

This last category of questions is associated with irreducible risk.

In a random culture, people are often punished when sound risk fails. The emotional temptation to punish sound risk that fails can be powerful. Leaders have been known to fire teams, sully reputations, and place blame liberally elsewhere when sound risk fails. When they do this, they usually find themselves increasingly isolated from the idea flow (and the "deal flow") essential to ongoing success.

When the rest of the company sees that sound risk that fails is punished, fear spreads like wildfire across the organization and *nobody wants to risk*. Creativity grinds to a halt, the organization becomes stagnant, and growth and profits start to decrease. It takes a particularly disciplined leader to avoid the indulgence of punishing sound risk. The best leaders are those who are best at this practice.

There will always be some irreducible risk, but we can minimize that risk—and the fear that surrounds it—by giving people solid principles on which to base decisions about whether or not to take the risk. We can give them guidelines for when to jump and when not to jump. This is how the best leaders operate.

Incidentally, it is also how the best venture capitalists operate. They understand the notion of sound risk and focus their investment decisions accordingly. Under the surface, venture funding is actually quite conservative. Rather than the shoot-from-the-hip frontier style often mistakenly associated with West Coast firms, venture capitalists usually use a cautious style that carefully delineates all the sources of risk and proceeds only where the uncontrollable risk is minimal. The result is that only about one out of every one thousand, or even five thousand, proposed ventures gets funded.

You may need to devise a way to analyze the risk involved in any proposal, to assess that risk by uniform standards, and to suggest how much risk is acceptable, under what circumstances. This is called dilemma analysis, and it's simply a way to decide whether or not to take the risk. Every risk boils down to a number of dilemmas. The more guidance you can give people in analyzing and making choices about those dilemmas, and the more you are willing to refrain from punishing sound risk taken in accordance with these guidelines when that risk fails, the more vital and innovative your organization can be.

Risk usually triggers fear. The bottom line is, many of your Trust Model guidelines will be antidotes to fear—directly or indirectly, consciously or unconsciously. A guideline to make no pretended commitments, for instance, helps to eliminate fear that people won't do what they say they will do. A guideline that dictates tact and respect in communication mitigates the fear of speaking up because of how others will react. If people are afraid to tell you their ideas for fear of being shouted down, denigrated, or rebuffed in some way, they will clam up and you won't have access to their ideas, disagreements, and innovations.

Fear is at the bottom of most negative emotional interactions, and people often become fearful in the presence of risks. When you include Trust Model guidelines about how to handle risk, you can nip a large percentage of that fear in the bud and prevent it from ever developing into behavior that can cut into profits, growth, productivity, and personal satisfaction.

## Phase 3 at Bigger, Inc.

As you recall, the lead team at Bigger was composed of Sam, Jan, Pat, Alex, Ted, Max, Randy, and Sheryl. Step 1 of this phase was crucial for this particular team and resulted in the deeper level of understanding necessary for them to work together. In doing the "Ten Questions for Leaders," each person saw how he or she had contributed to the stalemate at Bigger. This was a revelation, because each had secretly thought that he or she was blameless or the victim of other people's incompetence or animosity. When the lead team read "Ten Leader Tips for Building Trust," many of them saw themselves in the "before picture" that led directly to mistrust.

As they began to resolve open issues and clear away muck, the team got a much clearer picture of how the company had gotten bogged down. One factor that everyone discovered in himself or herself—and began to see in the company as a whole—was *risk aversion*. When Bigger had owned the market, a sense of entitlement had grown up across the company. Not only did the company think it was entitled to that huge market share, but individuals began to think they were entitled to regular promotions and substantial salary increases— whether or not they actually performed well.

Hand in hand with this sense of entitlement came an attitude of "Don't rock the boat." Don't make mistakes, don't take risks. Just keep things on an even keel. This attitude widened and deepened when people saw that the very few people who *were* willing to take risks were subtly punished when those risks failed.

So when Pat called Alex for those sales projections, he was willing to do almost anything not to give them to her. And when he was finally cornered and forced to hand them over, they were low and inaccurate. He didn't want to take *any* risk, an aversion that put the whole company in jeopardy not just because of the "Them vs. Us" dynamic it triggered with Pat, but because the company couldn't operate without sales projections. When Alex was *forced* to take that risk, he gave false information in order to minimize the risk. It was interesting that this incident, which triggered Bigger's crisis and caused them to seek help, was a microcosm of the larger dynamic of risk aversion that was crippling the company.

The team saw that, in addition to guidelines that covered growth, profitability, closure, commitment, communication, and respect, they wanted to include one that forbade punishing sound risk, and added a section titled "Sound Risk Guidelines." Next, they saw that to support these "Sound Risk Guidelines," they needed a section on "Dilemma Analysis" to help people analyze whether or not the risk was sound.

Here are Bigger's Trust Model guidelines:

### Bigger's Trust Model Guidelines

- We are committed to regaining the largest market share in our industry.
- We commit to raising profits by 20 percent over the next five years.
- We will close every communication.
- We will make no pretended commitments.
- We will communicate with tact and respect.
- We will not punish sound risk, as defined in the following "Sound Risk Guidelines" and "Dilemma Analysis."

### Sound Risk Guidelines

- Prepare for success.
- Convert risk dilemmas to recognizable goals.
- Note the "irreducible risk."
- Decide whether the "worst consequences" are survivable.
- When possible, consult people with actual experience.
- Devise pilots when appropriate.
- Do not drive choices by fear or loss or need for adventure.
- Achieve closure on forthcoming support.

### Dilemma Analysis

- With this dilemma, what are you trying to achieve? With customers? With Bigger? With your unit? With yourself?
- Identify your main fears, both "socially acceptable" and personal.
- What are the worst possible consequences for (*a*) taking the action and (*b*) procrastination? How probable are they? Could we survive them?
- How have you been investing energy into your dilemma? List both logical and illogical ways.
- How has "leadership" or the organizational climate played a part in the dilemma—positive or negative?
- How have you been participating in or prolonging your own dilemma?
- What could you do differently? When?
- What is the recognizable goal?

## Phase 3 at Startup, Inc.

Ironically, Startup's Trust Model guidelines also dealt in part with risk. As a hot new software company, Startup was *about* innovation—and innovation can't happen when people are afraid to take risks. It was crucial to keep creativity alive, and that meant not punishing sound risk.

After Randy, Damon, and Trevor had steeped themselves in trust principles, closed all the open issues, and handled the muck, they put their heads together to see what guidelines would foster innovation.

Early in Startup's history, a programmer had convinced Damon and Trevor to let him work for two months on a "revolutionary" new piece of software. It had failed to produce the results he wanted and had never gotten to market. He was fired. Since then, the only people who came up with new ideas were those who were willing to "put their heads on the block." In a field in which people change jobs frequently, make a lot of money, and live for the moment, Startup was able to find enough of these "heads on the block" people to keep going. But even Damon and Trevor knew that this phenomenon couldn't last forever, and that they had to create a culture in which risk was treated rationally. Startup needed a culture in which people could take sound risks without fear of being fired or punished. They didn't feel it necessary to add a whole section about risk to their guidelines, but they were careful to define sound risk.

Here is their complete set of Trust Model guidelines:

### Startup's Trust Model Guidelines

- We embrace change and innovation.
- We will resolve issues as quickly as possible.
- We will close all our communications, at every level of the company.
- We will only make commitments that we are willing to keep—no matter what.
- We will communicate with one another only with respect.
- We will each be responsible for getting our jobs done, but be willing to give and receive help.
- We will never punish risk that is taken soundly—which for you means in consultation with and with the approval of the CEO and founders.

- We will agree internally on what course of action to take before we discuss commitments to people outside the company.

When you have completed Phase 3 with the lead team, you are ready to take your Trust Model to the organization as a whole and get their buy-in in Phase 4.

# 11

# Phase 4: Commit the Organization

WHEN YOUR LEAD team is committed and has formulated your Trust Model guidelines, you can begin extending the Trust Model out into the rest of the organization.

Phases 1 through 3 occur only within the lead team. Phase 4 is about getting buy-in for your Trust Model guidelines from everybody in the company. There are two parts to this phase:

1. An initial kickoff meeting in which basic Trust Model concepts are introduced.

2. Smaller meetings in which you invite people to ask questions and offer input for the Trust Model guidelines. The guidelines work their way down through the organization, then back up again to leadership in an improved form that includes the combined intelligence of the entire team.

This kickoff and buy-in phase is the foundation for implementing the Trust Model in your organization.

The main issue you face in Phase 4 is *credibility*. People need to see and feel the specific benefits that the Trust Model will bring. When they do, their commitment will move from the head to the heart, and on out to the muscles. They will not only think about trust and feel good about your Trust Model, they will *act* on its principles and guidelines. And the more they act, the more they develop the habit of trust and automatically let go of old behaviors.

## The Kickoff Meeting

After you have buy-in from the lead team, the next step is to call a company-wide meeting. Contact all employees and tell them the purpose of the meeting. Let them know that you're going to talk about a new direction for the company, a direction that will benefit everybody by moving the organizational culture toward trust.

Your kickoff meeting can follow the same basic outline you used to obtain the lead team's commitment. Begin by describing the Trust Model and suggesting some of the benefits that other organizations have experienced by doing this—both the "hard" benefits of increased growth, profits, and productivity, and the "soft" benefits of more satisfaction, self-esteem, and enjoyment at work. Share with them your personal commitment to this path, and articulate some of the specific ways that you think the Trust Model will benefit your organization.

Give them at least a rough schedule for implementation, and let them know that you are going to invite their questions and seek their input in small group meetings. (If your organization is rather small, like Startup, Inc., this may be in the form of another company-wide meeting at a later date.) Elicit their agreement for this, and let them know that they will have ample opportunity in these small group meetings to voice their doubts, fears, and suggestions.

Ben owned an architectural firm that employed 150 people. To announce his kickoff, he sent a communication to all employees that the firm would close Monday morning for a meeting at which he would announce a "team and leadership development program based on trust principles." He listed the goals of being a trust-based leadership organization as:

1. to accelerate team achievement of essential business goals

2. to install a common foundation of high-performance teamwork skills throughout the operation that will enable individuals and teams to be more flexible, intelligent, and resourceful in achieving business goals

3. to develop a long-term competitive advantage through building a positive team culture that clearly focuses the team actions toward closure, trust, and supportive accountability

At the meeting, Ben described the Trust Model process and gave people a rough schedule for when and how he wanted to implement it. He told them about the small group meetings in which they would have a chance to ask questions and give their input into the Trust Model guidelines.

Then he said, "I am fully committed to this program, both as a tool to help accelerate our goals and as a vehicle to continue to make this a great place to work. We are seeking to avoid a quick-fix approach or mentality and instead to encourage a full commitment at all levels to this effort. Together we can make the difference that counts for each other and our customers." It was a great way to launch the program, and people had begun buying in.

Before the actual kickoff event, leaders may want to talk with some line people, supervisors, middle and senior management, and others to get a feel for how these employees see the problems in your organization. At the actual event, acknowledge the problems people are experiencing. Let them know that you are concerned as well, and share with them the process that the lead team went through in committing to creating a culture of trust. Review the timeline, and let them know what the next step is and how they can participate.

## Small Meetings: Getting Everyone's Buy-In

The next step is to get buy-in for your Trust Model throughout the entire organization. To do this, simply repeat the four-step process that the lead team has just completed, only in small focus meetings with the whole staff: (1) prepare with readings to be discussed at the meeting, (2) close open issues, (3) discuss the actual guidelines, and (4) ask for input and buy-in.

1. The leader, a lead-team member, or a designated outside facilitator meets with groups of up to forty people and reviews the basic trust concepts. The four steps used for the lead team can be repeated here: reading this book (or assigned parts of it), the "Trust: Ten Questions for Leaders" action plan, and the "Ten Leader Tips for Building

Trust." This information, and people's responses to it, are discussed at the small group meeting.

2. Ask people to list any open or unresolved issues. If these issues did not surface in the Phase 2 assessment, and were not among the open issues that came up for the lead team, begin the process of closing them. Issues that the lead team identified can be brought to these small groups for discussion. If they have already been closed by the lead team, you can report the results.

Disclosing these issues to everyone has several benefits. First, it demonstrates a willingness to confront open issues at the top and to resolve them with actions. Second, it provides a sanity check on the list itself, ensuring that the lead team is not stuck in "groupthink" while it denies other issues that are even more important. Third, it begins the tradition of open communication even before that specific element of the Trust Model has been discussed.

3. The draft Trust Model guidelines are then distributed for discussion. People are invited to comment and to make modifications. They are specifically encouraged to ask questions, voice fears, and suggest rewordings and adjustments.

At this point, you should expect skepticism. Many people have a history of mistrusting organizations, and so the content, emotional environment, and purpose of this meeting may be new to them. For you, the skills of listening, tact, and maintaining interest are essential. Hear and understand everything that is said. Use nonassumptive questions to probe further and invite elaboration. Remember, most input is not about you personally; it is simply the product of the person's fears. Answer questions honestly. If you do not know the answer, say so and always give a specific time for response. Let people know that you are in the same boat as they are when it comes to whatever irreducible risk exists in your situation. Help them understand that you share the risk.

It is useful to think of this step as a *validation test* rather than an exercise for formulating a new Trust Model draft. In other words, you want to invite people's input, but not encourage them to throw away everything the lead team has done. The facilitator may ask the group to imagine how your organization would look if people were actually adhering to the principles in the Trust Model draft. He or she might ask the following types of questions:

- If we adopted these principles, would we become the kind of organization you want to be a part of? (This is the *completeness* test.)
- Do any principles conflict with others? (This is the *coherence* test.)
- What could keep us from achieving full adherence to these principles? (This is the *feasibility* test.)
- How would we compare with other players in our industry if we adopted these principles? (This is the *competitive* test.)
- How willing are you to undertake the changes necessary to reach full compliance with these principles? (This is the *commitment* test.)

4. The facilitator then explicitly asks for group buy-in, recalling the difference between agreeing *with* and agreeing *to*. Again, it is not necessary to have unanimous agreement to the precise draft as long as *the consensus of the group* is in favor of this approach. Indeed, these groups usually include members who will never agree, in actual behavior, with these principles. They most likely will leave the organization over time as it becomes clear that acting out will not be tolerated in this environment.

At some point, you may want to include stakeholders other than employees in this process. These other stakeholders might include board members, shareholders, and sometimes even customers. Remember that whether you are dealing with employees or other stakeholders, the closer people are to the lead team, the more important it is to spend time eliciting their buy-in. People close to the lead team will need to model the Trust Model themselves and be leaders to the people who report to them. Another reason you may need to spend less time as you move away from the lead team is that, with each level of people you approach, you have more buy-in and agreement behind you.

This process is continued until everyone in the organization has been part of one of these small focus groups. The result of these meetings is consensus on a draft set of guidelines, which is probably much improved by everyone's input.

The lead team then ratifies a final version of your Trust Model guidelines and arranges to publish the results. They can also create reminders: write-ups for bulletin boards, posters, newsletters, wallet cards, etc. This entire process usually takes from a few days to a few weeks.

## Phase 4 at Bigger, Inc.

At Bigger, Sam held a kickoff meeting at which he announced the company's intention to establish trust as a guiding principle and outlined the benefit that he envisioned. He proposed a schedule and encouraged people to bring their questions to the small meetings.

Again, the questions that came up in the small groups generally fell into three categories:

1. **Those to which the lead team already knew the answer.** What's in it for me? How will it impact the conflict between my department and the other departments? It took quite awhile to sort through these questions because of the "Them vs. Us" history that had grown up at Bigger. The people running the small groups—Sam, the lead team, the outside facilitator—were patient. They welcomed and answered every question and concern.

2. **Those for which the team could get answers.** Can we get our European division to buy in? What happens when people violate the Trust Model? Will that be part of our performance review? Sam and the lead team said they would have to get back to people about the European division, and when they would do so, and asked people to suggest guidelines about what should happen when people don't attain closure or when they make pretended commitments.

3. **Those that the team could not answer now.** What if the market changes? This was something that no one could predict. While the lead team said that they were committed to the Trust Model regardless of market changes, no one could guarantee the success of the company. This was an irreducible risk, and the lead team let people know how they all shared it.

## Phase 4 at Startup, Inc.

At Startup, the company-wide meeting took place in one room. It already *was* a small group. Randy, the CEO, laid out the Trust

Model concept, set a schedule, and asked people to do the reading and self-assessment prior to a second meeting—to which people would bring their questions and input.

Startup's thirty employees were mostly aggressive, informal people who had a stake in the company and its success. They tended to be lean, mean rebels who worked hard, had a lot riding on what they did, and could go across the street and get more money in a second. When Randy stood with Damon and Trevor at the follow-up meeting, these folks asked him a lot of tough questions. Luckily for Startup, Randy knew just what to do. He expected skepticism, welcomed even the toughest questions, was happy to surface everybody's doubts and fears, and found it easy to tolerate criticism.

The questions fell into the three categories described earlier:

1. **Those to which the lead team already knows the answer.** Will there be training on how to reach closure with particularly difficult personalities? Will we learn what the best systems of communication are for long-distance: E-mail, phone, or getting on an airplane? Randy, Trevor, and Damon could answer "Yes" to both of these questions.

2. **Those for which the team could get answers.** Where will we get the modest financing needed for training? What will happen if there is an individual who does not wish to go along with this? Randy said he didn't have ready answers to these questions, but that he could find out. He promised dates by which he would get back to the group on each issue.

3. **Those that the team could not answer now.** What if the market changes? Again, this was something that no one could predict. While they could stay committed to the Trust Model regardless of market changes, no one could guarantee the outcome. Randy, Damon, and Trevor acknowledged that they couldn't predict the future, but made it clear that their commitment was constant and they were willing to share the risk.

At the end of the meeting, Randy asked for everybody's help, suggestions, and buy-in. He said that leadership couldn't do it alone, and that earned trust had to be a company-wide endeavor. He, Damon, and Trevor could establish the atmosphere in which trust could grow. They could provide resources and training. But he made it clear that they needed everybody's support in order to make a trust-based organization—and they got it.

At the end of Phase 4, you have buy-in both for the basic idea of making trust the focus of your organizational culture, and for the specific Trust Model you developed for your company. Now it's time to put your Trust Model into action and see how it works.

# 12

# Phase 5: Maintain Your Trust Model

DEVELOPING YOUR TRUST Model and getting people's buy-in are only first steps. Even more important is maintaining your Trust Model guidelines over time. To do that, you need ongoing assessments of how well it is working. You may need to make modifications in the guidelines, and you certainly need to keep encouraging trust across the organization and acknowledging its success.

Phase 5 is about converting commitment into changed behavior. If people's behavior doesn't change, you don't get the results. Remember, mistrust and nonclosure are just habits. When people see that they get better results by developing new habits, it will be easier for them to change their behavior.

The issue in Phase 5 is maintaining the integrity of your Trust Model so that it keeps getting stronger. The objective is to keep the flame burning—to assess how well your Trust Model is working over time, make any necessary changes, and to continue building a culture of trust.

## First Reactions

When you first begin using your Trust Model and people see that it is not just theory, but something real that affects how they interact with one another every day, they sometimes react with fear or disbelief.

They may say, "This is too idealistic; it'll never work." They may tell you that in business, you can't expect people to trust one another. This Trust Model thing can't be implemented, they may conclude. Nobody will buy it. Nobody will be able to do it. So thank goodness, they won't even have to deal with it. Everybody can just go back into their foxholes and start shooting at one another again.

This disbelief is often just a mask for deeper fears. It can be overcome by consistency. No matter what people say or how they react, you keep modeling trust and sticking to the Trust Model guidelines. People will either come around, or they will leave.

The more common first reaction to the Trust Model is fear—fear of change, fear of failure with these new skills, fear of exposure because everybody now has to come out of hiding and speak up, and fear of increased accountability. There may also be fear of loss. It's uncomfortable to give up the familiar old habit of buzzing, for instance, and the cherished beliefs about why it's "Them" and not "Us" who are causing the problem. People who have a habit of being victims will be uncomfortable with the new call to taking the initiative. The guidelines will probably pinch everybody just where it hurts most—in their bad habits.

The Trust Model asks us to let go of dynamics that were only holding us back and to become adults. Part of us hates this call, and that part of us sometimes tries to wiggle free. But we can't have the impact or recognition that we want to have, we can't make the contribution that we're here to make, or experience the deep satisfaction of true connection without playing our part.

We're being asked to make an investment, but that investment is blue-chip. It will bring us great returns on many fronts.

## What to Do with Resistance

Even after the Trust Model has been in place a while, you will be tested. People will have their reactions, and some of these reactions may result in resistance to the whole idea of the Trust Model.

Sometimes this resistance takes the form of overt, direct challenges. These are refreshing and can be handled directly. Simply be open and direct. Answer questions honestly, continue to model trust principles, and keep holding the vision.

You may find that someone on the team tries to use the Trust Model to further his or her own agenda. At one midsize manufacturing company, someone used the Trust Model as an opportunity to excoriate another team member whom he had never liked—both verbally and via E-mail—in the name of open communication. When we pointed out to him that he got an *A* in direct communication and flunked the part of the Trust Model that dealt with tact and dignity, he got the point that trust was not just one course, but a full curriculum.

Passive resistance is far more difficult to deal with than resistance that is direct and "in your face." Some people may just sit and wait—for someone else to move first, for you to shift your attention to some other initiative, for all of this to just blow away. This works a bit like the Tragedy of the Commons in economics, in which individuals exploit a shared resource to their own advantage and the group's detriment. Pollution is an example of the Tragedy of the Commons. It occurs when, for instance, a company releases emissions into the air in order to reduce its own cleanup costs. Most of us have experienced the Tragedy of the Commons at group dinners where you split the bill and people who have ordered thirty-dollar dinners pay the same as those who have ordered ten-dollar dinners.

With the Trust Model, we sometimes encounter a kind of inverse Tragedy of the Commons, in which people *don't* do something they are asked to do—to the detriment of the group. When this happens, it requires extra effort from everybody else just to maintain the status quo and drains the group's energy.

What can you do when the Tragedy of the Commons emerges? You can encourage people to speak up in new ways, to begin to change their habits, and to overcome fears that they may not have recognized until now. If you simply let people lean back passively, without participating or moving the process forward in some way, the whole team winds up sitting in the starting blocks. It takes encouragement, support, a safe environment, and all the skills of good listening and questioning to inspire this early movement.

While the Trust Model guidelines are still new to people, you may have to spend some extra time handling slippage and the new level of accountability. Two of your most powerful tools will be the Seven Steps to Closure (Chapter 6) and the use of *supportive accountability*. This term combines the notion of being supportive and nonjudgmental with the idea of full accountability. You hold people accountable for their promises, but not in a judgmental or demeaning way. "Supportive accountability" means asking, "What happened?" instead of "You screwed up *again*?" when there is slippage, and then dealing with people in a way that encourages change rather than retribution, discipline rather than punishment.

## Using the Resources You Already Have

Maintaining Trust Model guidelines sometimes teaches old institutions new tricks.

Human resources departments often seem to have evolved out of a vague instinct that people were important and that there ought to be somebody working on that. In fear-based random organizations, however, HR often becomes the "enforcer" of fear-based principles and dynamics. Hence the label "HR cops." Human resources people are frequently among the most sensitive folks in the organization, but they almost always end up shouldering the unresolved conflict between human needs and business demands. Many random leaders actually see HR's job as manipulating human needs to meet business demands.

The Trust Model offers a new opportunity for HR, a role that is both human and a resource. HR can become the leader and center of competence for building your trust-based culture, acting both as a conscience and as a guide. HR people can take the lead in understanding and articulating the principles of trust and the Trust Model guidelines, and the business advantage that they provide. They can also head up Phase 5, assessing how the Trust Model guidelines are working and acting as administrators of any changes that are necessary.

Human resource people can be the third-party monitors of what is actually happening as people start using the guidelines. They may be able to hear more clearly than leadership can what is being said—and not said—in the ranks. They can dig under the surface for what is really going on and what people really think. HR can actually lead the leaders, teaching them about what works and does not work, and helping them to see into their blind spots. It can also bring in additional resources from the outside and help build bridges between teams. Human resources can have a field day with the Trust Model.

# Creating Your Maintenance Program

The mechanisms for maintaining your Trust Model are limited only by your imagination. And again, human resources or an outside facilitator can play a vital support role. Following is a sampling of some ideas that have worked well for our clients:

- Establish regular contact to track how well the Trust Model is working. Set criteria by which you measure progress, and do an ongoing assessment of the status. Identify actions, goals, and other means to assess progress. Begin with the lead team's meetings. Experiment with how to make these meetings most effective, and then replicate the format for teams throughout the organization.

- Create a program that communicates about the Trust Model on a regular basis. Start by exploring the Trust Model guidelines in more depth, then provide updates with evidence of progress, anecdotes, and success stories. Begin with staff, and then reach out to all stakeholders—including customers.

- Create a formal Trust Model training program for new hires as a normal part of orientation.

- Imbed the Trust Model in the hiring process as recruiting criteria and as a competitive edge in recruiting.

- Conduct 360-degree reviews on an annual basis, where people on all sides—up, down, and across—contribute to the assessment.

- Build proficiency with trust principles into the performance review process and then into the incentive system.

- Implement an E-mail system whereby people can be at their desktop and still participate in a broad self-assessment session.

- Create an E-mail address for running commentary and suggestions on Trust Model progress. Make it possible for everybody to contribute and to read the results. Insist that management respond to any issue within a determined period of time.

- Coordinate periodic company- or division-wide communications from leadership.

## What Does Success Look Like?

Everybody in an organization needs to have a clear idea of what success looks like. One of the biggest obstacles to any transformational process is that people do not recognize success when it happens, and therefore cannot build on it. Confucius said that if you don't know where you are going, any path will get you there. We say that if you don't know what the destination looks like, you'll never know if you've arrived.

The early indicators of success with the Trust Model will be internal. They may include the following.

- hallway chatter, but this time about closure
- reduction in buzzing, with an uptick in brainstorming for closure
- people admitting mistakes and not looking as if they are about to die
- more ideas flowing from the bottom up
- fewer pretended commitments and quicker correction of those that do happen
- shorter meetings, with more closure, less infighting, and more energized and spirited discussions leading to new ideas and better directions
- more creativity
- more enthusiasm about work
- a change of vocabulary and an associated growing awareness about trust dynamics
- more voluntary commitments and an internalization of commitments—and real effort to meet them
- proud descriptions of changes to outsiders
- tasks getting completed, more and more by the original time commitment
- meetings starting on time
- less whining

Your job is to recognize these signs of success and acknowledge them. Any way you want to do this is appropriate, and you will come up with better ideas than any outsider ever could. Remember that this is a continuing process. Don't stop the acknowledgment after the first few times. Keep everybody moving toward the next success.

## Phase 5 at Bigger, Inc.

The lead team at Bigger decided to put human resources in charge of maintaining the Trust Model guidelines. It was an excellent choice, both because HR is a logical division to fulfill this function, and also because it gave Ted, the human resources director, a new lease on his investment in Bigger. You may recall that Ted could rarely be found in his office and often disappeared either literally to the golf course or metaphorically behind "all the work." It wasn't that he didn't want to do a good job; he simply felt hopeless about being able to make a contribution within the context of Bigger's former random-organizational culture. He felt overpowered by the "Them vs. Us" dynamics, the mushrooming fear, and the seeming inability of anyone to reach closure on anything.

The Trust Model guidelines gave him hope, and he became one of their strongest advocates. He was delighted when Sam, the CEO, gave him the job of making sure they were working, mediating problems that came up around them, assessing their impact, and suggesting changes when and where needed.

Since much of Bigger's Trust Model dealt with handling risk, Ted developed the following assessments of how well the guidelines were working.

## Organizational Climate on Risk

Please rate the following statements according to your opinion based on your experience of the organizational climate within Bigger, Inc. Use the scale provided.

| | |
|---|---|
| Strongly agree | +2 |
| Agree | +1 |
| Neutral or don't know | 0 |
| Disagree | −1 |
| Strongly disagree | −2 |

_____ 1. Sound risk taking is rewarded within Bigger.

_____ 2. It is all right to admit mistakes within Bigger.

_____ 3. My manager encourages me to take risks.

_____ 4. A failure on a sound risk will not be penalized.

_____ 5. My team tolerates controversy well.

_____ 6. People feel safe expressing disagreement at Bigger.

_____ 7. Risk takers get ahead in Bigger.

_____ 8. It is easy to get support for new ideas.

_____ 9. The organization provides resources to back innovative initiatives.

_____ 10. Bigger's leaders are modeling the way on risk taking.

## Individual Tendency Assessment

Read each statement. Rate each comment according to what level of risk you would personally perceive in taking each action within your current work group at Bigger, Inc. Use the scale below.

| | |
|---|---|
| No risk involved | −20 |
| Small risk involved | −10 |
| Don't know | 0 |
| Some risk involved | +10 |
| High risk involved | +20 |

Write the corresponding number from the scale above next to each item. I am willing to:

_____ 1. disagree with my boss on an important project

_____ 2. admit a mistake in a team meeting

_____ 3. give negative performance feedback to a peer

_____ 4. ask for help when I should already know

_____ 5. deal with an angry or upset customer (internal or external)

_____ 6. oppose a popular team decision I feel is wrong

_____ 7. make the final decision on a visible project

_____ 8. accept a new assignment with significant added responsibilities

_____ 9. challenge a decision I think is unwise or "political"

_____ 10. ask for acknowledgment when it is deserved

_____ 11. express anger or other strong feelings at work

_____ 12. say no to a customer (internal or external)

_____ 13. approach a second-line manager to resolve a conflict

_____ 14. approach a customer (internal or external) to resolve a conflict

_____ 15. delegate a key task on an important project

_____ **Total your "score" and divide by 15. Enter that number here.** _____

These assessments gave Ted a good idea of how people's behavior was changing as a result of living within the Trust Model. It told him who was becoming more productive and who was having trouble. It told him exactly where adjustments needed to be made and gave him some documentation when he went about making them.

Over time, Bigger flourished under the Trust Model and did regain its market share. And the people who worked there began to enjoy the benefits—both emotional and economic—of being with a leadership organization.

## Phase 5 at Startup, Inc.

Startup's assessment process was fairly simple, and Randy kept it within his own office. Every six months, he asked people to complete the following form, and made changes as needed:

## Assessing the Trust Model

1. How would you rate the importance of each guideline in making Startup
   a better place to work? Please check one box for each guideline below.
   The numbers mean the following:

   1. Not important
   2. Little importance
   3. Neutral
   4. Fairly important
   5. Very important

## Startup's Trust Model Guidelines

We embrace change and innovation.

☐ 1    ☐ 2    ☐ 3    ☐ 4    ☐ 5

We will resolve issues as quickly as possible.

☐ 1    ☐ 2    ☐ 3    ☐ 4    ☐ 5

We will strive to close all our communications, at every level of the company.

☐ 1    ☐ 2    ☐ 3    ☐ 4    ☐ 5

We will only make commitments that we are willing to keep—no
matter what.

☐ 1    ☐ 2    ☐ 3    ☐ 4    ☐ 5

We will communicate with one another only with respect.

☐ 1    ☐ 2    ☐ 3    ☐ 4    ☐ 5

We will each be responsible for getting our jobs done, but be willing to give
and receive help.

☐ 1    ☐ 2    ☐ 3    ☐ 4    ☐ 5

We will never punish risk that is taken soundly—which means in consultation
with and with the approval of the CEO and founders.

☐ 1    ☐ 2    ☐ 3    ☐ 4    ☐ 5

2. How would you rate your satisfaction that the Startup team (managers and workforce as a whole) is consistently using each guideline every day? Please check one box for each guideline. The numbers mean the following:

   1. Undecided
   2. Poor
   3. Average
   4. Good
   5. Excellent

We embrace change and innovation.

☐ 1   ☐ 2   ☐ 3   ☐ 4   ☐ 5

We will resolve issues as quickly as possible.

☐ 1   ☐ 2   ☐ 3   ☐ 4   ☐ 5

We will strive to close all our communications, at every level of the company.

☐ 1   ☐ 2   ☐ 3   ☐ 4   ☐ 5

We will only make commitments that we are willing to keep—no matter what.

☐ 1   ☐ 2   ☐ 3   ☐ 4   ☐ 5

We will communicate with one another only with respect.

☐ 1   ☐ 2   ☐ 3   ☐ 4   ☐ 5

We will each be responsible for getting our jobs done, but be willing to give and receive help.

☐ 1   ☐ 2   ☐ 3   ☐ 4   ☐ 5

We will never punish risk that is taken soundly—which means in consultation with and with the approval of the CEO and founders.

☐ 1   ☐ 2   ☐ 3   ☐ 4   ☐ 5

Part IV has given you a step-by-step method for implementing your Trust Model. Whether you follow these steps exactly, or find new ways to implement your Trust Model, the result will be a new culture of earned trust in your organization—one that you can adjust as needed to create an environment in which greater closure, productivity, growth, profitability, commitment, and satisfaction flourish.

## Part V

# BEYOND THE
# TRUST MODEL

# 13

# The New Face of Leadership

As WE HAVE seen throughout this book, trust-based leadership demands new skills. The most important job of any leader is to breathe life into the connected team, and into the trust that binds that team together and creates its competitive advantage.

## The New Amalgam

In a trust-based organization, leadership is a form of emotional custodianship and requires the qualities of connectedness, relatedness, empathy, expressiveness, instinct, and compassion. These right-brain qualities join with traditional, rational left-brain business skills to make up the core of this new type of leadership.

Many of today's leaders have not been trained in the emotional aspects of high-performance team life. In business schools, the emotional content of teams is often given lip service but not effectively addressed. Yet emotions are at the core of any team. To produce extraordinary results, we need to understand how such emotional dynamics as trust, fear, dignity, and meaning operate on teams.

Fast-track leaders sometimes have a difficult time letting go of the idea that traditional leadership skills such as strategy, systems, structure, and quantitative analysis—those on which they believe their early success was based—are the only "right" ones. They tend to focus on choosing the right side of the issue, rather than on converting "Them vs. Us" and other negative interpersonal dynamics into closure and discovering an even better answer.

In an organizational development class at Stanford, students were given a choice of two case studies on which to work. The first involved a complex portfolio investment problem requiring sophisticated financial-risk models; the other involved allocation of parking spaces in the company parking lot. The MBA students leapt on the former like hyenas on fresh meat. The Sloan Fellows, on the average ten years older and more experienced, chose the parking space allocation problem. They knew what the really important issues were and had more experience in dealing with emotional situations.

Preoccupation with left-brained technique may actually mask a reluctance to delve too deeply into one's own emotional life, which is a prerequisite to understanding others. Being willing to engage in self-examination is the only way to achieve authentic growth, and that kind of authentic personal growth is crucial to the new leadership.

We don't seek to preempt traditional business abilities with these "softer" skills, but to create a new balance and a new order of effectiveness. We want to combine professional acumen and the ability to read financial statements with an understanding of people and skill with relationships, interpersonal dynamics, social capital, and internal currency. We are looking for more than just small incremental improvements in what we already know. We want a leap into the unknown that will bring benefits beyond what we thought possible.

## Personal Development

While the effort may be great, the rewards for this form of self-development are both profound and unique. We can move our careers along through maneuvering, politics, or plain dumb luck, but without personal growth, we become increasingly dependent on circumstances. Real, dependable career progression requires that we grow as people, so that all parts of our internal system evolve together in balance.

Being connected to the team also means being connected with ourselves, and being able to convey to others what is really going on with us. People can sense if we are not being entirely honest with them, or if we are trying to be something we are not. They see and remember when we put our own ego needs above those of the team or other team members. Conversely, appropriate expressions of authentic emotion—fear, enthusiasm, anger, frustration, boredom, hurt—can do more to create a connection than the best intellectual argument.

Over time, our own internal connection with our instincts and emotions provides a source of intelligence that augments the intellectual. It is as if our intellect sits at the gateway between the external situation and our internal gut response. We consult first one, and then the other, to gain an authentic consensus. The head finally recognizes the potential contribution of the heart, and we let all capacities work together to produce a new order of results.

## Closure as a Leadership Skill

We have seen after working with hundreds of groups that beyond survival needs—food, shelter, safety, etc.—the strongest urge felt by teams is for resolution, or closure.

Early philosophers identified *limbus partrum* as a special place between heaven and hell for those not good enough for eternal bliss yet not deserving of eternal punishment. Limbus became limbo, the first circle of hell in Dante's *Divine Comedy*, an excellent primer on unenlightened team life. There Virgil explains, "We are lost . . . we live desiring without hope." In other words, there is no closure.

The leader of today needs to master the specific skill of closure, along with those skills that facilitate it—listening, resolving "Them vs. Us" dynamics, nonassumptive questions, etc.—in order to liberate the team from despair and to sustain hope. Lead us not into equivocation, but deliver us from limbo.

## Integrity

Integrity is another essential leadership quality. There is a great deal of literature on the subject of integrity and its value for business, but we like to focus on the root word *integral*, which means wholeness and implies structural soundness. It's easy to draw an analogy between the elements of structural soundness that computer network managers seek and the elements sought by great leaders. These elements are connection, information flow, lack of delay, error correction, uptime, and reliability. "Buzzing" is to a team as a virus is to a computer.

Integrity means holding the team to sound principles of operation and performing continuous quality checks. The more stakeholders who are included in this process—boards, suppliers, partners, and especially customers—the greater will be the leveraged effect of trust.

Leading from trust inevitably requires that the leader not just perform honest acts and not tell lies, but that he or she be an honest person. This honesty includes the "simple variety"—filing complete and truthful tax returns, correcting the salesclerk when he or she tries to give you too much change, and returning lost wallets stuffed with cash.

Integrity also includes "difficult honesty"—honesty with and about oneself, and the courage to confront how we may be part of the problem. Integrity is letting go of our justifications and explanations of why it's the other person's fault, or the system's fault, or just plain "their" fault, and looking again to see where the responsibility is truly our own. It is moving in the other person's direction until we are sure we have crossed the 90 percent responsibility marker, and knowing that we still really may be only halfway there. This self-scrutiny can't be just an intermittent task; it has to be a way of life. This kind of honesty goes way back to our ancestral admonitions to know ourselves, and we realize that all our modern labor-saving inventions cannot spare us this task.

## Asking for Help

If we want the team to function at its highest level, we also need to model asking for help. This may be leadership's greatest potential contribution.

Many leaders are more comfortable offering help than asking for it from people who report to them. Some of us may hold limiting beliefs about help, ideas such as:

- Leaders should know what they are doing at all times, or else why are they leading? That's why they're paid the big bucks.
- Asking for help reveals weakness, and accepting help puts me in debt. Next time, I'll have to pay back dearly.
- I must need help desperately, and be in dire straits, before I can ask for it. I must be needy before I can approach

anyone. It's not okay just to want help as a means of reaching extraordinary productivity.

- If I need help, I'll have to reveal secrets and share credit.
- If I accept help, I won't know how to thank the giver.

But not asking for help is hoarding—hoarding of need, of problems, and of opportunity. These are not helpful. Embracing problems as opportunities is the best way to transcend our limits and enhance our abilities. Asking for help is a way for leaders to give to their teams, and is almost always a gesture of generosity.

## Modeling Trust: The New Leader's Primary Role

The primary role for the new leader is to model the principles of the trust community that he or she leads. This usually means just getting out of the way, rather than obscuring the view by waving pom-poms. You become more like a pane of glass than a billboard. Your task is to keep the window clear of power games, so that the team can see through to the light beyond.

It's important to be clear with people that *you* are not the principles. You are merely organizing a coherent *focus* on them. Avoid the pedestal. Let people know you understand that we are all human beings, leaders and team members alike. At times we all feel incomplete, worried or fearful. From time to time, we all wake up in the dark hours in a cold sweat, wondering if we can hold it all together.

Still, you are the one whose job it is to keep the energy flowing toward a coherent center of values. And fortunately, there is a specific way to do this. Nothing creates energy like listening, caring, and offering a set of operating principles that is recognized as universally attractive. If you genuinely care about people, authentically want their input, live the Trust Model guidelines, and give people the information and training they need to live these guidelines themselves, then you are doing everything you can to create a culture of trust that benefits everybody in your organization.

This kind of caring and listening brings into the organization a principle that successful leaders have always used with customers. While it's important to give the customer what he wants in terms of goods or services, careful listening and caring about his needs is just as important. This listening and caring is what creates the initial closure with customers. The result is an energy flow *from the customer to the company*. The same principle operates with your employees.

We're not talking about the old kind of "listening and caring"—the talk-your-ear-off, glad-hand, hold-on-to-your-wallet charisma that some people associate with sales. Rather, what we're getting at is making an unquantifiable but deeply felt impression. We may not remember what people told us, but we never forget how they made us feel. Within the organization itself, this kind of listening and caring with employees tells people that you're not just giving oozy praise designed to manipulate them into cheerfulness, but real support in stretching them to what they can really become.

## Going Deeper

Most of us are familiar with traveling in a horizontal direction when it comes to work, but very few of us dig vertically to mine our work lives for personal depth as well.

In our business lives, we urgently want to get somewhere, and so the horizontal routes are well-traveled. We know how to move forward, clear a path, blaze a trail, leapfrog, seize a beachhead, stake out new territory, and turn around. But we often miss the opportunity to learn lessons that teach us about ourselves and help us become better people, as well as better managers. In business, it's sometimes acceptable to have personality—but not soul.

The result is that our business lives can be like Spanish moss—green and verdant, but without roots, depth, or solidity. We cannot reach real depth when we let fear of exposure, risk, or loss stop us. It's safer to think of ourselves, and let others think of us, as economic units executing value-added functions with compensation calculated to match. We begin to leave our values, our longings, and our yearning for transcendence at home, and to enter the workplace wearing the armor of our persona. But there is only limited satisfaction along that path. Sooner or later, we get tired of it.

Making trust the centerpiece of our organizations means that we must learn something about the vertical pathways and move downward toward those layers that we have been avoiding. We must become like a sturdy oak rather than like Spanish moss. Our roots need to go deeper, and we need to be tall and strong enough that people can depend on us. There we find emotion and heart and passion, and liberate a new kind of energy, profitability, and meaning.

## The New Leaders

The new leaders are self-aware and genuinely involved with their teams on more than superficial levels. They know how to create environments in which people can make the contribution they want to make and be as productive as they can be. These new leaders understand the emotional energy that drives teams to extraordinary performance, and they are skilled at focusing people's attention on the trust principles of closure, commitment, and genuine connectedness based on respect.

They know how to use the most powerful force on earth, human energy, in a way that is clear and focused. They drive a culture in which people want to bring their best to work, and reap the emotional and economic rewards of doing so.

In doing these things, the new leaders achieve an extraordinary level of growth and productivity, and give their organizations a competitive edge. These are the people who will be most sought after in the coming years, because they are the ones who produce the best results, bring the highest levels of satisfaction, and are able to draw the best people to their organizations. And these are the leaders who will be most richly rewarded, both financially and personally.

# Index

# About the Authors

## Arky Ciancutti, M.D.

Dr. Ciancutti's interest in trust and effective teamwork grew out of his work as an emergency department physician. He noticed that "Them vs. Us" dynamics often arose between doctors and nurses, between nurses and med techs, and between health care deliverers and hospital administrations. He also noticed that this distrust communicated itself to patients—who felt out of control when they arrived, and then saw that they had been thrown into (or "landed in") a situation that was also out of control.

Ineffective communication, confusion about priorities, overlapping efforts, and other fear-based dynamics were not conducive to healing, so Dr. Ciancutti realized that he needed to learn about trust. His research identified the components of successful, trusting working relationships. He began teaching teamwork and stress management— "preventive medicine"—in 1973.

In 1974, he founded The Learning Center to further research the components of successful working relationships. It became the first organization to provide team-building to business and health care communities. He and his organization have worked with teams ranging from startups to Fortune 100 boards of directors.

Today, Dr. Ciancutti is director of Learning Center, Inc. (learn ingcenter.net) in San Anselmo, California. He is also the founder (and gardener) of The Brewery Gulch Inn in Mendocino, California, where he conducts teamwork and leadership workshops for executives.

He has taught teamwork and change at the Sloan Program at Stanford University's Graduate School of Business. He is the first nonemployee in IBM history to teach the IBM Basic Beliefs (Respect for the Individual) to management. He developed and delivered the course on Change Management for IBM and in 1993, he supplied IBM USA and IBM International with a turnkey risk-management system. He also developed turnkey systems and customized courseware at the Boeing Company, Applied Materials, and many others. He designed and facilitated the Financial Improvement Process at the University of California San Francisco Medical Center, through which employees themselves trimmed $25 million in overhead.

Dr. Ciancutti has addressed senior management groups including Novell, Exodus Communications, Women.com, Soar (San Francisco 49ers' physicians), Elan Pharmaceutical, the Federal Reserve Bank, Utilicorp, Ford Aerospace, Stanford Research Institute (SRI), WorldRes.com, Fox & Carskadon, Interop, Lynch Enterprises, Chevron, Dexter, and many more. In 1999, he won the Speaker Achievement Award of TEC, an international organization of CEOs.

He has made many media appearances—local, national, and international.

A graduate of Swarthmore College and Case Western Reserve University School of Medicine, he completed his specialty training in pediatrics at the University of California Medical Center in San Francisco.

His books include *The Emergency Care Handbook* (Lancaster, Pennsylvania: Techonomic Publishing Company, Inc.) and *The View From the Gurney Up* (Lancaster, Pennsylvania: Techonomic Publishing Company, Inc., 1984), widely reviewed as the "classic" for understanding help exchange interactions in health care.

# Thomas L. Steding, Ph.D.

Dr. Steding has had more than twenty-nine years of technical and executive management experience in building and developing high technology companies. His interest in trust and teamwork grows out of his pragmatic involvement in building high-performance teams in intensely competitive, fast-changing environments. He has been working with Dr. Ciancutti in multiple team environments since 1983.

He is currently president and CEO of Metacode Technologies, Inc., providing software infrastructure products for the next generation Web. He was president and CEO of RedCreek Communications, Inc., a hardware Internet encryption and security startup. He was a founder, president, and CEO of Pretty Good Privacy, building on the most popular software encryption program in the world. He was vice president and general manager of the Communications Infrastructure Division at Novell, comprising $150 million in revenue and over 300 staff.

Dr. Steding held a number of marketing and general management positions at 3Com Corporation, including vice president and general manager of the Enterprise Systems Division, formerly Bridge Communications, Inc. He held senior executive positions at Sony Microsystems, a Unix workstation organization in Sony America, and at Ardent Computer, a graphics supercomputer startup. He was executive vice president and member of the board of directors of Systems Control, Inc., acquired by British Petroleum in 1981.

Dr. Steding has extensive media and public relations experience, including television, radio, general business press, and computer industry press exposure.

He has degrees in electrical engineering from the University of Michigan, a Ph.D. in electrical engineering and computer science from the University of California, Berkeley, and an M.S. in management as a Sloan Fellow at the Stanford Graduate School of Business.